UP AND RUNNING:

OPENING A
CHIROPRACTIC OFFICE

Dr. John L. Reizer
Dr. Steven L. Reizer

UP AND RUNNING:

OPENING A
CHIROPRACTIC OFFICE

ISBN 1-930252-70-6

Published by Page Free Publishing, Inc.
733 Howard Street
Otsego, MI 49078

UP AND RUNNING:

OPENING A
CHIROPRACTIC OFFICE

Dedication

This book is dedicated to the future chiropractors of the world.

Table of Contents

About the Authors

Dr. John Reizer is a December 1986 magna cum laude graduate of the Sherman College of Straight Chiropractic. Born in Lakewood, New Jersey in 1963, he returned home to his native state after graduating Chiropractic College and opened up two successful chiropractic offices. Dr. Reizer returned back to South Carolina and his alma mater as a member of the Sherman College faculty in 1998 after 12 years of private practice. Dr. Reizer currently practices in the Sherman College Health Center where he supervises interns who are preparing to enter the field of chiropractic. Dr. Reizer resides in Inman, SC and is married to his wife of 10 years, Melissa Reizer. They have a daughter named Kayla.

Dr. Steven Reizer is a March 1996 summa cum laude graduate of the Sherman College of Straight Chiropractic. Dr. Reizer also holds a Bachelor's Degree in accounting from Georgian Court College in Lakewood, New Jersey. Born in Lakewood, New Jersey in 1967, he currently operates a successful chiropractic practice in Boiling Springs, South Carolina. Dr. Reizer is also a member of the Sherman College faculty where he is an instructor in the clinical science department. Dr. Reizer resides in Inman, SC and is married to his wife, Beth Reizer, who is also a chiropractor. Dr. Reizer has a daughter named Olivia.

Introduction

CONGRATULATIONS! You have just graduated from four very tough years of Chiropractic College and have just passed all of your licensing examinations. You now have that all important piece of paper in your hand that allows you to begin the next challenge of your professional life. . .a practice.

If you are like most of the recent graduates that we have met over the years you are probably overwhelmed by the thought of opening up a chiropractic practice on your own. You have most likely heard a number of different theories about which way you should proceed. Some of your fellow classmates will try out positions with established doctors as associates because they feel they lack the proper business skills to step out on their own right out of school. Others will hire a coach or a guru for many thousands of dollars who will preach to them about making a fortune in their first year. Others will simply go out blindly and will dive right into an office setting learning the hard way that practice can be rough if you do not know what you are doing.

When you were a student in Chiropractic College the pressures of running a business and making an income from chiropractic were not present. You had other pressures to manage in the way of school work and clinic requirements. These were legitimate stresses that haunted you throughout your college education. Now the stresses of college life have been replaced by the stresses of practice life. College life has also left you with financial debt which will carry over to your practice life, and so it is very important to start out your practice in an intelligent way. You do not need to get further into debt.

Since being affiliated with a chiropractic college as instructors, we have had numerous students approach us about which way they should start out once they become licensed. This anxiety that most chiropractic students seem to have usually begins a short time after they enter the clinical portion of their education. The anxiety seems to escalate up until they graduate and then peaks after licensing examinations have been passed.

Because we are in the teaching field we have decided to write this book to help you get your practice up and running properly right from the very beginning. We do not believe that students, already submersed in debt, should continue to get further into financial distress.

We are not saying that a coach or consultant who charges $5,000-$15,000 a year cannot help you grow a successful practice. For some people this is a viable option. They require someone to push them every step of the way. They cannot seem to get out of the college tuition mode which they have been associated with for the last eight years. We do feel however that you can save a lot of money by reading our book and by following the information that we have outlined. This is good material that we have picked up throughout the many years we have been practicing. We will not charge you thousands of dollars for the information either. We also will not ask you to pay us 15% of what your practice earns for the first three years that you go into business.

What we will explain to you in this book will be so valuable to your practice life that you are going to want to send us thousands of dollars to thank us. We will not accept your money. We want you to take the money you save by reading our book and reinvest it into your business. We want you to be successful. We believe that your success is important and very good for our profession. When chiropractors fail in their practice lives people who need chiropractic care ultimately must pay the price.

It is our sincerest wish that this information will be of great help to you. We would like nothing more than to remove the fears you may have of opening up a chiropractic practice and to replace them with the confidence of running and operating a successful business.

Dr. John L. Reizer
Dr. Steven L. Reizer

Choosing a Practice Type for You

WHEN chiropractors get ready to set up a practice the first thing they must do is to decide on the type of practice they will be implementing. This is one of the most important decisions you will have to make and it is a prerequisite that must be completed before any other decisions are determined. The type of practice that you set up will determine many of the additional choices you will be making later on down the road.

Choosing a practice type that is right for you is a personal choice that only you can make. Obviously it is a decision that must fit within the personality and the makeup of each and every practitioner. We do not wish to pick and choose for you a specific practice type. What we will do at this point is to list and cover the different practice variations that we feel are most representative of the profession today.

THE FAMILY WELLNESS PRACTICE
THE PEDIATRIC PRACTICE
THE GERIATRIC PRACTICE
THE SPORTS PRACTICE
THE PERSONAL INJURY PRACTICE
THE WORKERS COMPENSATION PRACTICE

THE FAMILY WELLNESS PRACTICE

The family wellness practice objective is to maintain a variety of patients of different age groups through a lifetime commitment of chiropractic wellness care. This type of practice is probably the least stressful and the most rewarding because of the long term relationships that are often established with patients. Some important considerations that the doctor should think about include the need to have a higher volume practice and possibly a lower fee schedule. Because you will be offering, to a large extent, wellness/ maintenance services, many of your fees will probably not be eligible for insurance reimbursement. Doctors that have this type of practice usually see a large volume of patients on a given day.

When we enter into a wellness practice we will see less stress in our everyday practice routine. Almost everyone that you will see will be there for subluxation correction only. Education by the staff and yourself will be paramount in keeping your patients on purpose and returning for care on a regular schedule. Later in this book we will discuss in detail patient education and how it should be applied in regards to this type of practice setting.

THE PEDIATRIC PRACTICE

The pediatric chiropractic practice objective is to create awareness in the community about the importance of chiropractic care for children and to maintain the spinal health of patients at an early age and then throughout their adolescent years. For the most part we are talking again about a subluxation based practice. Special equipment and seminar training may come in handy for this type of practice scope. In most situations however, the basic knowledge you have learned in chiropractic college is more than adequate for taking care of children. The pediatric practice also requires a special personality type on the part of the practitioner. Children can certainly present challenges and even the need for modification of techniques, at times, which should be definitely taken into consideration. The doctor must exercise extreme patience when working with children and be understanding and tolerant when faced with the various moods that these younger practice members sometimes exhibit in the office setting.

THE GERIATRIC PRACTICE

The geriatric based practice objective is to provide spinal care for the elderly patient. The patient in this age group characteristically will present with multiple subluxations and often associated degeneration of a very advanced phase. Many degenerative changes of the spinal column must be dealt with and careful analysis along with specialty techniques may need to be utilized. Because of these obstacles the time that is often spent with each patient could be quite lengthy.

We feel that it would probably be a very good idea for a practitioner contemplating this practice specialty to consider learning a number of low force techniques. Low force percussion instrumentation would be helpful in this type of practice.

It is also advisable to contact a medicare consultant to help you understand the necessary and current regulations regarding the medicare program before you start to see any patients.

There are many regions within the United States that have heavily populated areas of senior citizens living in retirement communities. If your office location is in close proximity to such an area the possibility of developing a very successful practice in this category would be outstanding. It has been our experience to witness a number of these successful practice types in different parts of the country and especially in the states of New Jersey and Florida.

THE SPORTS PRACTICE

The sports based practice typically deals with sports related injury. Depending on your own philosophical background, this practice can be subluxation or injury site based. Most chiropractic offices that have devoted their practice objective to athletes tend to concentrate a large amount of their time on symptom and injury related complaints. Again, special training, analysis, and techniques are often necessary for this type of practice objective.

Professional team sports such as football, baseball, basketball, soccer, and others are now employing and placing on staff chiropractors to maintain the spinal well being of their very highly paid athletes. There are many exciting possibilities to consider regarding chiropractic in the sports related arena.

THE PERSONAL INJURY PRACTICE

The personal injury practice is devoted to patients that have been injured usually in motor vehicle accidents or on someone's personal property or real estate property. This type of care is almost always corrective in nature and culminates in about 2-4 months. The patient is usually released after the conclusion of treatment and the doctor is expected to write a narrative report and possibly appear in court for expert testimony regarding the patient's future prognosis relating to the possibility of future permanent injury. In almost all of these patient cases an attorney is retained by the patient and litigation will take place. Very accurate record keeping by the chiropractor is necessary.

It is advisable to check the current laws regarding personal injury care in the state which you plan to practice in. Various states have different laws governing the way personal injury care can be practiced. The laws are constantly changing and you will need to keep up with such changes on a regular basis.

It will also be necessary for you to develop a narrative report format so that your report writing for these cases will be handled expeditiously. We have included in this book (in the forms section) a copy of a sample narrative report that you may feel free to utilize, modify, for your own use in your practice.

THE WORKER COMP PRACTICE

Workers compensation based chiropractic care is devoted to patients that have been injured at their place of employment. Again care is going to be provided for a shorter period of time that will ultimately culminate in the release of the patient from your care at the conclusion of the authorization time stipulated by the employer. It will be important to always make sure that before you begin any care on these types of patients that a written record of authorization, from a company official authorizing care by you, be presented to you and kept in the patient's permanent file. Without this authorization form you will not be able to legally take care of such patients and cannot receive reimbursement from the company or their insurance company covering the injury claim. We have included in this book (in the forms section) a number of sample forms that will need to be used for this type of patient in this practice setting. You may feel free to utilize, modify these forms for use in your practice.

Many of these different practice types can be operated within a subluxation based theme. It is always the individual chiropractor who will decide what their overall objective in practice will be. The choice that you will need to make is which one of these practice settings best fits within your comfort zone. For many young doctors out of school this is an easy decision which they have made long ago. For some doctors this decision warrants careful thought and research. Many practices across the United States probably have a blend of more than a few of these practice types wrapped up into one practice. Once you have made up your mind on the type of practice you want to open, you will be ready to proceed to the next logical step in this process which is to find a good location for your office.

Finding an Office Location

Just about any business person you ever talk to will tell you that having a good location is essential to the success of any business. Some businesses have a good location in a catalogue. Their source of business might be mail order sales. Another company might have a terrific location on a "search engine" on the internet because they are doing business through the World Wide Web via computer sales. A pizza shop might have a good physical location for their business in a mini strip mall with tremendous visibility from the road. No matter what the business service is, it must have a very good location in relationship to the intended client base that it is trying to attract.

A chiropractic office must also have a very good location in regards to the client base it is trying to address. The right location for your office will depend somewhat on the type of practice you have chosen to operate. As we wrote in the last chapter, proximity to certain segments of the population (retirement communities, professional sports teams) might play a slight role in where you decide to set up. There are however, some common sense items to consider when deciding on your office site. Remember, once you pick the spot, you have to live with it for a while. Here are some ideas to help you with your decision process.

TRAFFIC VOLUME

The volume of traffic that passes by your proposed practice location must be healthy. You do not want to be situated in an area where there is minimal traffic. The best business locations are usually the spots with the highest traffic counts in the city or the township. When you begin to look for office suites for rent you often will come across advertisements for business property that will state that their location is in a "high traffic count" area. These offices are usually considered prime locations to lease and they usually are priced higher than locations with less traffic flow.

SIGN PLACEMENT

It is extremely important that the location that you choose affords you the right to place a very visible sign in front of your office that can easily be seen and read by the traffic volume that is passing by. There are many office locations that can be found on major highways that do not allow for proper displaying of a business sign. These locations should be avoided because they will make your practice invisible. When you get ready to place your signature on your office lease be sure that within that agreement it is clearly stated in black and white that a large prominent professional sign will be placed in front of your office in order to attract patients.

Make sure that your sign is visible from the road and position it in a place that will get maximum visibility from traffic coming from both directions. The sign should include your office name, chiropractor's name, and office phone number. The sign should have colors that will grab the attention of passing traffic, such as red letters on a white background or a blue and white color combination. The sign should be professionally designed by a sign company. Explain to the manufacturer what you are looking for. Let them show you different samples so that you are sure of what you are getting. Also be sure to get several quotes from different sign companies. You will be amazed at the wide range of prices that will be given to you. This will ensure that you get the best price in town.

ACCESSIBILITY TO YOUR OFFICE

It is very important that patients can get into and out of your office location with ease. This means that the patients can easily turn into your office from the road and can exit in both directions without having to worry about getting into a traffic accident because of an obstructed view of oncoming traffic. If this is the case, do not lease the office space. Patients will not want to come to your office. They will associate that traffic obstruction with you and there goes the patient.

It is equally important that patients have easy access to your office once they have made it in from the roadway. Your office should be on the ground floor unless there is an elevator provided in the complex. Patients should not be made to climb up or down sets of stairs to gain entrance to your building. Your office should also be clearly marked with professional sign markers indicating your exact location in lobby and foyer areas. This is especially true in the case where there are numerous practitioners leasing space in a professional office complex.

PROVIDE ADEQUATE PARKING

Make sure that the location you choose has enough parking spaces to handle all of your patients. It is a major headache for a customer / client to go into a place of business and not be able to find a place to park their car. If you want to lose patients, this is a good way to go about doing it. Depending on how long you take with your patients and the way you choose to schedule them will ultimately determine how much parking your office location will require. On average, an office should provide enough space to accommodate at least 7-8 automobiles at one time. The parking lot should be paved with asphalt or cement. A dirt lot or a lot filled with loose rocks and stones is not a good idea. Patients do not want their cars and trucks getting dirty and scratched up whenever they come to see you. Remember, your entire office setting should be inviting and convenient for your patients. We do not want you to lose customers before they even get to your front door.

Another important factor that needs to be considered is proper lighting of your parking lot. If your office hours are going to take place at night you need to make sure that your parking lot is illuminated to a sufficient degree. Patients have to feel safe getting in and out of your office. You do not want patients tripping in your parking area because they cannot see due to a lack of proper lighting. Make sure the lights to your parking area are on a timer and work properly for your patients' safety.

A SAFE COMMUNITY

A very important consideration regarding your office location is whether or not the area appears to be safe from crime. If the site you are looking at looks unsafe to you it is going to look unsafe to your patients as well. You need to find this information out before you sign a lease. It is obvious that no place in this country is completely safe from crime although, there are certainly places that appear to be safer than others.

If you are new to an area and have limited experience in a town or city it would be very wise to contact the local police department to talk with someone about a specific location. In the process of buying or renting a home to live in you would certainly do some research about the prospective community. One of the things you would want to probably know about is the crime rate in the immediate vicinity. Your office location should be no different. It should be part of the homework you do in researching your office location. If you have lived in a location for a long enough period of time that you have a sense of how safe or unsafe a place is your research will be very easy. The advice we will give to you is to stay away from places that you know are trouble spots. You will have a difficult time building a practice in such a locale.

IS THE COMMUNITY GROWING?

Is the area that you are considering for your professional practice a growing part of the community? When you look up and down the street do you see evidence of the community expanding in a business sense? Can you locate other businesses nearby your office site that are doing well? These are all very important questions that you will need to ask yourself before committing to a lease agreement.

If you see an area that has a lot of run down properties with various companies going out of business, this is not a very good sign. This would be indicative of a town or community that is dying. You do not want to open a new chiropractic office in a community that is contracting or dying. You will often find very low priced rental property in these types of towns. Stay away from these locations. This is a disaster waiting to happen to you. We have seen several chiropractor friends make this mistake and then have to close their businesses down after a year or so. This is a no win situation and you will end up paying a costly price for your bad assessment of the area.

If on the other hand the community is expanding and other businesses are doing well and you see evidence of continued expansion in the near future, this would be a positive sign to proceed.

Office Space And Layout

The amount of office space that is needed to create a chiropractic office is determined entirely by the individual doctor. It is important to consider a number of factors however, in coming up with the right individual answer for every new practitioner. Many young chiropractors make the mistake of leasing too much space and therefore have unnecessary overhead. The office space that will ultimately become your practice should be functional space. For example, you do not want to lease a one thousand square foot office and have half of the floor space as storage. This would be a waste of office space and you would be paying a fortune for square footage that was actually not needed. Here are some of the key items to think about:

HOW MANY DOCTORS IN THE OFFICE?

If your practice is going to include a multi practitioner setting with several different chiropractors utilizing the same office at the same time it will be necessary to have a substantial amount of office space. In order to ensure proper patient flow within the office you must make sure that each practicing individual has a minimum of at least one room to service incoming patients. If the number of doctors exceeds the number of available rooms there could become a patient backup problem as the practice grows down the road.

If your practice is going to consist of only one chiropractor, yourself, you probably will only require between 700 and 1000 square feet of professional office space. Any space in excess of this amount is probably going to be excessive on your part and a waste of your hard earned money.

HOW MANY PATIENTS CAN YOU SEE AT ONE TIME?

No matter what type of practice style you have, you can only concentrate and adjust one patient at a time. Certain practice settings with an open room atmosphere can allow you to see one patient at a time a lot quicker and therefore allow your volume to flow more efficiently. Some doctors have a preference for closed room adjusting with only one patient in the adjusting environment at a time. Whatever your professional personality may be it will be important to consider these tastes in the assessment of how much office space you will actually need.

In the case of an open atmosphere practice, a much larger examination/ adjustment room is going to be utilized. Volume efficiency is going to cost you overhead for larger amounts of square footage.

In the office where there is only one patient being present in the examination/ adjustment room at a time the space requirement will be greatly reduced. Volume inefficiency will save you overhead expense by reducing amounts of square footage required.

HOW MUCH EQUIPMENT WILL BE
NEEDED IN THE OFFICE?

Depending on the technique and analysis package you decide to use, your equipment needs may be very large or very small. This is a very important consideration in trying to calculate the amount of office space you will need. If you need to put an x-ray machine in your practice site with a processor to develop films in a timely manner this will require additional office space, electrical wiring, lead lined walls and doors. If you plan on using a radiologist for your x-ray needs the space you will need is decreased.

Most chiropractors will probably place one or two chiropractic adjusting tables in their office. If you are providing physical therapy or additional services which require equipment, the need for additional space will go up.

HOW MUCH WAITING ROOM SPACE IS NEEDED?

Chiropractic offices tend to move their patient volume rather swiftly and so therefore a large waiting room is usually not going to be a necessity. Again this is a generalized statement that can be different for every office depending on the scope of practice being performed by the doctor. We suggest that a good safe number is about 10-12 waiting room chairs in about 120-144 square feet of office space. These numbers are an estimate and may actually be slightly larger or smaller for your own personal needs. The nature of a chiropractic office is to perform routine wellness based care. Unlike a medical office where there is quite a bit of waiting for the doctor to perform lengthy examination procedures, chiropractors have their patients examined, adjusted and on their way in a short period of time. The actual amount of time the patient is in the waiting room is miniscule compared to other types of professionals in the healing arts.

HEATING AND COOLING THE OFFICE SPACE

The larger you make your office the more overhead it will cost you to heat and cool it. Utility bills will be a factor in your overhead expense. Depending on what part of the country you will be practicing in, heating and air conditioning bills can eat up a lot of your profits. Our suggestion to you is to try and minimize the actual amount of office space that must be climate controlled. Keep electric and gas bills to a minimum by only creating as much office space that is needed to function properly.

CALCULATING THE COST TO LEASE AN OFFICE BY THE SQUARE FOOT

When you see an advertisement to rent professional office space it is usually written in a format that explains how big the office is in terms of square footage. Square footage is calculated by multiplying the width of a building by the length which will = square footage. If you have an office that is 30 feet wide and 40 feet in length you would have a 1,200 square feet office.

Professional office space is also advertised in most situations by listing a dollar amount per square foot. An advertisement might state the following:

```
*************************************
Professional offices for lease:
Builder will subdivide 15,000 SF into 1,000
SF office suites. $12.00/SF
*************************************
```

What this advertisement is telling you is that a total of 15,000 square feet of office space is available for lease. The owner is willing to subdivide the entire 15,000 square feet into office suites of 1,000 square feet each. The price of the office lease will cost $12.00 per square foot for the entire year. 1,000 square feet x $12.00 = $12,000 for the year. It will cost the doctor $12,000 to lease that office location for one year payable in twelve monthly installments of one thousand dollars per month.

NEGOTIATING THE LEASE

A very valuable secret that many people are not aware of is that the asking price in real estate is never written in stone. Most people will haggle over the asking price of a home but not over the asking price in a lease situation. Office lease prices can be negotiated. Sometimes you get a better price and sometimes the owner or leasing company will hold firm in their position. Regardless of the outcome it does not hurt to test the waters and try to get the price down.

We suggest that you stay away from a *Triple Net Lease*. A

triple net lease is an agreement to lease a property by making a monthly rent payment based on a square footage calculation like we just explained and additionally to make payments on common area maintenance fees and property taxes on the building. The additional fees are charged to you on a monthly or semi annual basis and represents your proportionate share of the entire buildings complete property tax bill and common area maintenance fees. Your proportionate share is calculated by the amount of square footage you lease. So if you agree to lease 1,000 square feet of a 15,000 square feet complex you will be assessed one fifteenth of the overall expenses.

The type of lease that you want to agree on is a straight lease where just the square footage is paid for. You do not want to pay any other fees. Also try and get the electric and water included in your lease payment. This is done all the time and landlords will give you this if you complain loud enough.

In addition to this, tell the landlord that you want to sign a one or two year lease only with an option to sign a longer term lease at the end of the initial lease with only a moderate to small increase in rental price. What this will do is to protect you against a long term locked in lease that you cannot get out of. If you do it our way you can still have the security of a long relationship with the property but just in case the location does not work out for you there is an escape route after a year or two. The option to re-sign gives you a chance to execute a long term lease at the same price and if you want out of the property at the end of the first year or two you do not have to exercise your option to re-sign and away you go to a better location without financial penalty from the landlord.

DESIGNING AN OFFICE LAYOUT

The chiropractic office layout is very important and should be given some considerable thought. Do not finalize any blue prints until you have carefully gone through all possibilities. Remember, simplicity is a wonderful thing. Keep the design and layout very functional for the type of practice which you will be running. What might be functional for one practitioner might be very non functional for another.

The office floor plan should allow for a smooth patient flow of entrance and exit traffic. An office should consist of a waiting room, reception area, adjusting room(s), x-ray and processor room, lavatory, consultation or doctor's office, closets, and a storage area. In the front part of your office you might want to place the waiting room, lavatory facility and the reception area. In the middle portion of the design many doctors will place the adjusting rooms and doctor consultation office. In the back portion of the office is a good place to locate x-ray equipment, closets, and storage areas.

You might also want to consider having a foyer entrance if your office exit goes directly outside. This can prevent wind gusts from blowing through your office. If your office suite is an internal unit amongst other offices you will not have to consider a foyer.

Make sure that your adjusting rooms are large enough to contain your equipment and allow you ample room to move about in order to examine and adjust your patients. The adjusting room should be at least 10x12 in size (about 120 square feet.)

When designing the reception area, many doctors will choose

to create an open area that coexists within the boundaries of the waiting room. This is a friendlier atmosphere than concealing the receptionist in another room behind the security of a sliding glass door. The reception area can be built within the waiting room space by the creation of a counter top style island. This is a very popular design that seems to work well for many chiropractic offices. One flaw in this type of design is that some people do not like to discuss financial business and payment arrangements in front of other patients. Depending on how you set up payment transactions with your patients, this may or may not be an acceptable design for you. Most doctors and patients find this design very comfortable. We personally think that this design is a good fit for a chiropractic office.

The doctor's consultation office should be designed a little larger than the adjusting rooms to create an impressive yet comfortable atmosphere for the doctor and patient. Important patient –doctor communication and education will take place in this room so it has to be large enough to place a nice desk with a chair for the doctor and two chairs for the patient and usually a spouse. Also allow space in this room for a book case that can be filled with professional text books and other items you might want on display in the room. This is also the room where you will want to place your diplomas, degrees and awards that you have earned in your professional studies.

Your x-ray and processor room should be about the size of an adjusting room. Most equipment can be placed very conveniently in about 144 square feet. When you lease or purchase your machine be sure to ask the company what dimensions would be most beneficial for proper operation of that unit.

Other areas of the office are less important in their dimensions and can be designed to fit each individual's personal preference. Storage space, lavatory room and closets all fall into this category. Keep in mind that if you have more or less space to work with all of these dimensions can be modified accordingly. It is advisable not to go too large and not to go so small that you cannot operate properly.

Buying Or Leasing Equipment

The decision to purchase or lease certain types of office equipment depends on the type of practice you will be running. The equipment which you acquire must be able to allow you to properly complete your professional practice objective.

There are some important factors that every young chiropractor should understand before heading out blindly to furnish their office with tables and x-ray machines. We would like to make you aware of some of the different options that could possibly be available to you that might help you to get exactly what you need for the least amount of overhead. We would also like to point out some of the features on certain types of equipment that may or may not be important in your office depending on the practice type you elect to use.

STATIONARY VS HI-LO TABLES

The decision to use a stationary table versus a motorized one to transport your patients from a horizontal position to a vertical angle is a matter of personal preference. Since most people that come into a chiropractic office can usually get up and down on their own, without much assistance, a stationary table works just fine. Many doctors will have one table of each variety just in case a patient that has difficulty with movement comes into their office. If you know that you are going to specialize in a geriatric practice you might want to consider a motorized table.

Motorized tables are going to be much more expensive than stationary tables and depending on the make and the model, the price difference could be quite significant. We suggest that you cost compare the many different brands and models on the market regardless of which direction you decide to go.

TABLE FEATURES

Chiropractic tables can come with a number of different optional features. The best optional features for you to have installed will be based on your technique specialty. We feel that the most commonly installed choices are drop mechanisms in each of the major spinal regions. Other features such as intersegmental traction, specialized cervical drop mechanisms for specialty techniques such as *Thompson* and *Pierce* are also somewhat common. There are a number of other items that can be customized on tables such as horizontal motorized lifts that can bring the patient higher or lower in the horizontal plane. There are tables that can have their drops loaded manually or automatically by a foot pedal. Chiropractic tables will usually have a cervical head piece that will hinge up and down creating states of forward flexion and extension in the cervical spine. The thoracic region should have a "swing down" option that will allow the dorsal spine to sag slightly if desired. Most tables should have a foot rest that can be raised or lowered for the performance of leg check analysis or to position the feet into a higher or lower elevation to reduce stress on the spine during certain adjusting procedures.

Tables can come upholstered in vinyl, leather, cloth and probably other coverings. Depending on what selection you go with, prices can be expensive to relatively low in cost. We suggest that individuals just starting out save money and go with very durable lower cost coverings. If taken care of properly they will last a very long time and the replacement fee, down the road, is inexpensive.

X-RAY UNITS

The decision that you will have to make regarding an x-ray machine is whether or not you want to incur the expense of having one placed inside of your office. The other viable options are of course to use an outside radiologist, or not to take x-rays. Depending on your technique and analysis methodology, you will choose one of these avenues. If you decide not to x-ray, the decision process is obviously removed. If your technique requires x-ray utilization you will have to decide on in house or outside services. Both can work very well in your practice. Our suggestion to new doctors is to utilize a radiologist nearby in the early stages of your practice and then buy or lease a unit once you are able to handle the expense.

Radiologists take very good quality films that can be screened for pathology by the radiologist before you even get the films in your office. You can then concentrate on the chiropractic analysis portion of reading the films and you can still charge a professional chiropractic reading fee as a service which you are providing to your patient.

LEASING VS BUYING

Once you have decided on the type of equipment to place in your office you will have to decide whether to lease or buy it. There is no scientific proof that shows one way to be better than the other. If you decide to lease your equipment over a period of time you will technically be renting it. If you decide to purchase your equipment you will take ownership of the property immediately. Our advice to new doctors is to study the pros and cons of both options and then make a decision that is right for you.

Leasing is a very sensible way for professionals to obtain their office equipment. Many young chiropractors cannot afford to purchase twenty or thirty thousand dollars worth of tables and an x-ray unit when they come right out of school. A lease agreement over a five year period of time, with small monthly payments, is an attractive and logical way to manage this overhead expense. Most agreements to lease office equipment will permit the chiropractor to purchase the property at the end of the lease period for one dollar. In reality you are actually financing your equipment and not renting it. For income tax purposes however, the lease agreement will allow you to deduct the entire twelve monthly payments off of your total income for the year. If you pay a monthly lease payment of five hundred dollars, you will get a tax deduction of six thousand dollars at the end of the year for your business equipment.

There are many companies that have leasing programs set up for professionals such as chiropractors. Many of these programs will allow young doctors to have very small monthly payments for the first six to twelve months and will then increase the amount of the payments later on after they have had a year to develop their business. This type of leasing program is known as a "step up lease" and can be a tremendous help to a new doctor facing financial challenges.

Most doctors that enter into lease agreements in order to obtain their office equipment decide to acquire new property that is somewhat expensive. If this is the way that you are planning to go, leasing may be an option for you.

If you are contemplating the acquisition of second or third hand equipment that is not nearly as costly as equipment that is new, you might want to consider purchasing over a leasing program. The advantage in this situation is a drastic reduction in your monthly overhead and immediate ownership of the property. Whatever the equipment may cost you can also be deducted off of your income in the form of a tax deduction as long as the property is properly depreciated over a period of time. A certified public accountant can help you with depreciation laws regarding office equipment.

Our suggestion to new chiropractors is to keep your overhead down by purchasing older equipment that is in good condition and have it refurbished. A second hand table with new coverings can easily be mistaken for a new piece of equipment. The only difference will be the huge savings in your bank account. The same goes for x-ray equipment. Purchase an older unit and processor that are in good condition and save a lot of money. The savings can be used to pay the rent on your building for six months or longer. Remember to always try and keep your overhead down. Every dollar you save is a dollar less that you have to earn and be taxed on.

Picking A Name
For Your Office

Choosing a name for your office is probably one of the easier items to deal with in setting up your practice. Many doctors will simply use their own last name in this process and then add the words chiropractic center. This is quite acceptable and you never have to worry about someone having that practice name unless of course your last name is a very common one.

If you decide to use your last name there are a couple of ways you can do this. One way to accomplish this is to just call your office:

Dr. John Reizer
Chiropractor

This is very simple and to the point. Because you are utilizing your own name in the business trade name there is no need to register the business name with the township or county clerk's office. Another way to list your name as the business trade name would be:

John L. Reizer, D.C.

This is perfectly acceptable and keeps everything simple and free from the responsibility of name registration within the county or township as well. This is a smart way to set up your office name because checks and payments will be made out to you which is also the name of your business. You have the option of cashing these checks or depositing them into your business account. If the company name is something other than your own name you will be forced to deposit the check into a business account that matches the name printed on the check. For example:

Reizer Chiropractic Center

If a check or payment comes into the office payable to the Reizer Chiropractic Center, it must be deposited into the Reizer Chiropractic Center business account with that same matching name. The check may not be cashed by anyone including the owner of the business. If you are planning to have many different employees in your business handling incoming payments, you might choose to have your business name listed in this manner. This is an excellent way to guard against theft in your office. If on the other hand you are going to be a sole proprietor it is more convenient for banking purposes to list your name as the trade name and have your business account simply labeled as your own name as well. In this situation checks can be cashed immediately by you or they can also be deposited into the business account.

OPTIONAL NAMES

Some chiropractors will choose names other than their own last name for a number of different reasons. In certain situations an office might be located on a very well known street within the community. Because the street is a prominent landmark, that many people are very familiar with, it sometimes is wise to name your office after the street name. In reality, you have linked your office to a well known name without having to do any outside marketing. Your office will automatically become a well known landmark as well.

Other name choices can come from the name of the town, county, a special name that has important meaning about the mission of chiropractic, and even a name that begins with the letter "A" in order to get a great placement in the phone directory in front of all of the other office names that are further down the alphabet. If you choose an optional name you may have to register the name with the county clerk's office in your community. The reason this is done is to make sure that two businesses do not share the same exact name in close proximity or within the county.

In certain communities across the United States it is not necessary to register your business name with the county clerk. It is advisable to call the clerk in your area to see if this step in the process will be necessary for you. If this process is necessary for you to complete, keep in mind that it only takes a few minutes of your time to do so and only a nominal fee is charged for the name search and registration process. Once your business name has been registered and recorded by the county or township clerk you will be issued a certificate to present to the local bank in order that you can open up and establish your business account. Without the registration certificate from the clerk's office you will not be able to open up a business banking account unless you were to use your own name in the account listing. The certificate is necessary in order to use an alternate trade name on your account.

ESTABLISHING YOUR BANK ACCOUNT

Once you have secured your business name it will be necessary to secure a business bank account. This process will only take about a half hour of your time to complete. The first thing you should do is to find a convenient bank that is close to your office location. You will need to actually go inside of the bank to fill out a few papers and to make an initial deposit to open up your account. You will need to order a check register, business checks, and deposit slips from the bank as well. You will need a good supply of these items in order to be able to function as a business. The bank will ask you for the trade name you will go by. Give them the certificate from the county clerk that will authorize the use of the name you have chosen, or simply give them your own name and how you want it to appear on your account. On your account you will also need to place your business address or your home address. This is where your bank statements will be delivered. You will also need to place your office address on your checks and a business telephone number if one has been established. If the phone number has not been established at this point, tell the bank to give you temporary checks and delay the printing of your permanent checks until the phone number has been established.

ESTABLISH YOUR BUSINESS PHONE SERVICE

Your business phone number can be established right from your home by calling your local phone company. Pick up your local phone book and turn to the first couple of pages. You will see a page that explains how to do business with the phone company. You will need to call a special business number and the phone company will ask you where your office location is at. You will need to give them the exact address and office suite number in order that they can verify if service currently exists at that location and can be set up for you.

The phone company will ask you if you have a special number that you would like. Try and pick an easy number that is simple to remember. They will try to accommodate your request if they have that number available. If they cannot honor your request, ask them to read off some numbers that are operational and choose the best combination of numbers that will work at your location.

The phone company will ask you what your business trade name is. Always keep your business name consistent with everything else. The business phone number should be listed under the same business name that appears on your business bank account. Ask the phone company the earliest date that your name can be placed into the *Yellow Pages* section of the phone book. It is important to get your name listed in the business *Yellow Pages* as soon as possible. Tell them that you only want the minimum listing that is included within the price of your business line fee. We will discuss advertising advice along with phone book advertisements in a later chapter.

The phone company will ask you how many additional lines you will require for your office. Since each business line is going to cost you (depending on what part of the country you will be practicing in) approximately $50-$100 per month, it is advisable to hook up only one line initially. Tell the phone company agent that you want the following features placed onto your phone service.

1. Call Waiting.
2. Call Forwarding

Call waiting will alert you if someone is trying to call while you are on the line with someone else, and the other party calling will never get a busy signal. This is like having two phone lines for the price of one. Call forwarding can be used when you are ready to leave your office for the day and you want to have all calls coming into your office redirected to another number. Most doctors will forward their calls after hours to a cell phone or a message center.

Finally, the phone company will give you a date that your business line will become activated. Write the date down on a piece of paper and the work order number that corresponds to the activation date. Once you have confirmation that your number is working it will be safe to have your office number printed on your bank checks and other office forms.

BUSINESS CARDS

Now that your business name, location, and phone number have been established it will be safe for you to order business cards. Business cards happen to be one of the most important advertising tools you will ever create. A business card should be kept relatively simple and to the point. The design is based on your personal taste. A print shop or a company such as *Staples* or *Office Depot* can create thousands of business cards for twenty or thirty dollars. This is a very inexpensive investment. The store where you purchase these cards will also help you design the card.

Your business card should include your business name, the chiropractor's name, phone number, address, hours, and some services that you may provide. Also a logo can be placed on the card to identify your profession. Look at the example below:

Office Hours By Appointment   (LOGO)

Reizer Chiropractic Center
Dr. John L. Reizer
33 Main Street
New Egypt, N.J. 08533

Services   **Telephone: 609-758-1111**

Business cards are usually completed for delivery within 7-10 days. Once you have them in your possession you are ready to start advertising your trade name and business location.

Insurance You Will Need To Purchase

We are a litigious society! People in the United States like to bring about litigation amongst one another. This is a fact of life and it is a fact of our business life as well. The chiropractic profession is no stranger to lawsuits. Without proper protection your practice could be destroyed by such a legal action. It is vitally important for all chiropractors to protect their practices against such potential devastation by making sure that they are adequately insured.

There are three types of insurance products that a chiropractor will need to purchase. Two of the three types will need to be purchased before you open your doors to your first patient. The third type of coverage you can wait on until you can afford to purchase it.

The most important policy you will need to activate is professional liability (malpractice) insurance. You should not see any patients or offer professional services to anyone unless your professional liability coverage is effective and covering you. There are two different types of policies that are sold in this category of insurance. We would like to take this opportunity to explain both products.

CLAIMS MADE POLICY

A *Claims Made Policy* is the cheaper of the two different products. If you purchase a *Claims Made Policy* you are purchasing insurance protection against a potential lawsuit that may come about as a result of professional negligence on your part. The lawsuit will be defended by your policy up to the limits of liability written into the contract provided the policy is still actively in effect at the time that the legal suit is received by the insurance company.

Let us give you an example of how this type of coverage works. Suppose a chiropractor with this type of insurance policy has an act of professional negligence occur on March 4, 1999. The doctor is notified six months later in September that a lawsuit is being brought against their practice and that it becomes necessary to notify their attorney or malpractice insurance company of the action in order that a response can be sent to the plaintiff's attorney. In this situation the chiropractor went out of business in July of 1999 and cancelled the malpractice coverage effective July 31, 1999. This chiropractor has no coverage at the time the lawsuit was received and even though the coverage existed during the time the act of negligence took place, there will be no legal obligation by the insurance company to cover the doctor against the pending litigation. If the chiropractor would have kept the policy active after going out of business and the policy was active at the time the claim was sent into the insurance company, the suit would have been fully covered and the litigation would have been defended in full compliance with the policy limitations.

This type of coverage requires chiropractors to maintain the policy in an active state at all times in order for it to protect the doctors against future litigation. If a chiropractor wanted to retire the chiropractor must keep the policy in full force or the doctor must purchase a product called *Tail End Coverage*.

TAIL END COVERAGE

Tail End Coverage is a supplemental product that can be purchased by doctors who have *Claims Made Policies. Tail End Coverage* will protect the policy holder from any legal suit that may come in after the practice has closed and up until the statute of limitations for that potential act of professional negligence has passed. In most states a patient has up until two years to file a claim for professional negligence and after that period of time has elapsed a suit cannot be brought about by a plaintiff.

This type of *Tail End Coverage* is essential to have if you ever consider purchasing a *Claims Made Policy*. To be completely safe from litigation, a doctor must have a period of two years take place since the last date which he or she practiced. This is a long period to sweat out and *Tail End Coverage* eliminates the need for any further worry during that two year period.

AN OCCURRENCE POLICY

An *Occurrence Policy* will protect a chiropractor against an act of professional negligence provided the policy is in effect at the time that the act of professional negligence takes place. This type of policy is a more expensive policy than the previous product we discussed. In this situation a chiropractor may close his or her practice and not have to purchase an additional policy such as *Tail End Coverage*. Occurrence policies automatically have the back end insurance protection built into them. If the doctor terminates the policy the coverage still protects the policy holder during the entire time period the contract was active. If a claim for litigation is served to the doctor eighteen months later and the negligent act took place during a time when coverage was active, the doctor of chiropractic is completely covered and will be defended by the insurance company up to the full limitations of the contract.

It is our suggestion to doctors starting out to go ahead and purchase the *Occurrence Policy* so you have the peace of mind of knowing that you will always be covered without any lapse in protection. This is not an area that you want to fool around with.

LIMITS OF PROFESSIONAL LIABILITY

A limit of liability is the dollar amount of insurance protection the chiropractor is purchasing from the insurance company. Professional liability policies can be written with all types of limits of liability. The greater the limits of liability the more expensive the coverage will cost in the form of insurance premiums. Depending on the insurance company that is underwriting your policy, the limits of liability may be broken into three or four options. They are usually written in the following format:

Policy 1 $ 100,000/ $ 300,000.
Policy 2 $ 500,000/ $1,500,000.
Policy 3 $1,000,000/ $3,000,000.
Policy 4 $2,000,000/ $6,000,000.

This format is stating that in policy number 1 that a doctor is fully covered by either a *Claims Made* or an *Occurrence Policy* up to $100,000 for each incident of professional negligence. The doctor may have up to three different claims made against his or her practice in the same year and still have insurance protection for each individual act of professional negligence up to $100,000 each. The coverage will be limited to a maximum of $300,000 for all three acts of professional negligence combined.

It is our suggestion that you purchase a limit of liability of at least $1,000,000 / $3,000,000 for your own protection. If you are planning to sign up with health insurance companies such as *Blue Cross* and other major carriers so that you can accept health insurance plans for your patients you will need to have malpractice limits of liability in this range. Health maintenance organizations (HMO's) will usually require their participating doctors to carry malpractice limits of liability in the $1,000,000 / $3,000,000 level as well.

COMPANIES TO CHOOSE FROM

There are quite a few companies to choose from regarding

professional liability policies. We suggest that a doctor shop around for the best rates possible. Professional liability insurance for chiropractors is very affordable. This will not cost you a tremendous amount of overhead in comparison to the protection and security it will provide. Depending on the type of practice you operate and the professional services you render to your patients, the insurance premiums can vary from $400-$4000 per year.

Once you choose a company, they will send you a questionnaire to profile your practice type. Chiropractors that limit their scope of practice to subluxation correction can expect to get the lowest rates in the industry. Insurance actuaries have calculated subluxation based practices to be the least risky in terms of paying out claims.

NEW DOCTOR DISCOUNTS

Many insurance companies will give a 25% discount off of their final premium calculation for doctors entering their first year or two of practice. If the company does not mention this information to you, do not be afraid to ask them about this offer. In addition to this discount almost every company offers a 50% discount off of their final premium calculation for doctors that practice for twenty hours a week or less. This is known as the "Part Time Doctor" discount program. If you do not ask for these discounts the agents will not always inform you of them.

OFFICE LIABILITY INSURANCE

The second type of insurance policy you will need to

purchase before you start seeing patients is *Office Liability Insurance*. This policy will protect you against a potential lawsuit that comes about as a result of someone becoming injured in your office from a slip or fall or an accident in this category. These are accidents outside of professional negligence.

Most landlords will require that you have this type of coverage in effect before they will even let you sign an office lease agreement. In fact most lease agreements will have printed within the contract a stipulated amount of insurance that must be purchased naming the landlord as an additional insured. This type of coverage is going to cost anywhere from $350-$600 a year depending on how large or small your office is. These policies also have built into them insurance to cover your office equipment from theft, fire and other devastation. Again, it will be very important for you to shop around in order to secure the best possible rate for this product.

PROFESSIONAL DISABILITY INSURANCE

Disability insurance is not something you will purchase right out of the gate. This is a policy that is designed to protect the doctor from a loss of income in the event that the doctor becomes injured or sick and cannot operate a practice for a period of time or even on a permanent basis.

Most insurance companies that sell disability policies will want to see a copy of your tax returns for the past couple of years to see what kind of business income you have. An insurance company is not going to sell you a disability policy that will pay a doctor $75,000 a year if the practice is only bringing in $60,000. In this situation the doctor would be better off being disabled and so a policy would not be issued. If for example a doctor was making $100,000 per year on a regular basis, that doctor would most likely be able to purchase disability insurance up to about $75,000.

Although this product is not something that you will be concerned with initially, we thought that it was important enough to warrant a short discussion on the subject. Our advice to anyone with a practice is that this is a great insurance product and one that should definitely be considered if you can possibly afford it.

The premiums that are paid for this type of coverage are not cheap and they can be used as a business expense deduction. It should be noted however, that if the premiums are not utilized as a tax deduction for your business the payout on a claim (the income you receive when disabled) is not taxable by the federal government. If you choose to use the premiums as a tax deduction, claim payouts would be taxable. This is just information for thought and you should always consult with a certified public accountant before making tax decisions in case current laws happen to change.

Office Forms
For Your Practice

The careful design and production of office forms is a very important aspect of preparing to open your practice. The forms that you create will become confidential, legal documents containing essential information about your patients. This information will serve two primary functions. The first function will be to utilize the information in a way which will help you to assess the overall health picture of the patient. Forms in this category will also help to relay and transfer vital health information to other practitioners and to assist the patient in communication about their health conditions to employers and other essential outlets. The second function of this information will assist you in getting paid for your services. The forms in this category will collect personal information that is of a non health related nature such as street addresses, phone numbers, and insurance companies.

We would like to discuss in some detail the various forms that you should utilize in your practice. At the very end of this chapter we have included a section which will display each form that you will need in order to ensure the smooth operation of your business. You may feel free to use all of these forms verbatim within your own practice.

PATIENT REGISTRATION FORM

A patient registration form is used to gather information about the patient such as their name, address, telephone numbers, employer's address, date of birth, occupation, spouse's employer, social security numbers, referral information, sex of patient, and other non health related material which you will need to have in the patient file.

The form will also contain an area that will provide questions about method of payment and insurance information. Some of the insurance information you will want to collect will be the name of the insurance company and their address. You should also find out where to mail the claims to. Information such as group numbers, additional insurance coverage, subscriber's name, subscriber's relationship to patient, and subscriber's insurance identification numbers should also be recorded. The form should also have a section on "assignment of benefits" which will allow insurance payment checks to come directly to your office and not to the patient.

The patient registration form should also have a section that will allow you to note if the patient is coming into your office as a result of an accident of some type. The type of accident should be identified and any insurance information related to an accident should be recorded as well. If the patient has retained an attorney in conjunction with an accident the attorney's name and office address along with a telephone number should be placed on this form.

PATIENT HEALTH HISTORY FORM

The patient health history form is a very important part of your patient file. You want to have a document that is easy to read and easy to access information from. This form is going to ask the patient the reason for their visit, the date the problem began, type of pain or discomfort, a rating of how bad the pain is, frequency of the problem, and what activities does it interfere with. You should also ask on this form if other types of treatment have been rendered and if so by what doctor and the date that the treatment was administered.

You may or may not want to have a section on this form that will review various systems of the body. This is usually accomplished by having the patient check off any conditions that he or she might have had in their health history either current or in the past. Another option is to just ask patients to list any health related conditions or disease processes they may have had in the past or that they currently have.

This form should also gather information on the patient's work activity, exercise habits and recreational and lifestyle habits such as smoking, and drinking alcohol. Also it is important to determine if the patient has had serious injuries, surgical procedures, fractures and any other types of trauma. It is also important to record any types of medications the patient might be taking.

CONSENT TO CHIROPRACTIC CARE FORM

The consent to chiropractic care document is a "terms of acceptance" that you will want all of your patients to read over and sign. This piece of paper will explain to the patients what chiropractic is and how you will render professional services for them. When patients read and sign this form they are granting their consent to be patients in your practice. They have made a choice to undertake chiropractic care based on the terms and conditions which you have outlined in printed format.

It is important to include and briefly explain the procedures that you will be utilizing within the scope of their care such as the taking of x-rays, spinal adjustments, modalities, and any other phases of treatment you deem necessary for patients.

The consent to chiropractic care document should also have a place for the patient to sign at the bottom portion of the paper. An additional space should be made available for the legal guardian's signature in cases dealing with children that are under age.

SPINAL EXAMINATION FORM

The spinal examination form is going to be utilized in the recording of patient spinal data that takes place during actual patient examinations. The goal here is to create a customized form that is easy to use and is representative of the necessary tests and procedures you will be using in your practice.

Some of the items that need to be placed on this piece of paper are palpation notes and findings, subluxation levels, posture analysis, orthopedic and neurological testing, reflexes, range of motion and other findings that will be pertinent to your philosophical objectives. We are not going to try and convince you to practice, philosophically, in one direction over another. Our goal is to help you set up your office paperwork in a manner that will allow you to function in a smooth manner no matter what philosophical direction you gravitate towards.

RADIOGRAPHIC REPORT FORM

If you are going to take x-rays in your office you will need to create a form that very neatly categorizes all important radiographic results. The information on this document should be divided into four different spinal sections. The cervical, thoracic, lumbar, and pelvic regions should each be formally examined with the results being recorded on this form.

A radiographic commentary on curves, curvatures, osteoarthritis, osteoporosis, and other degenerative changes should be included in this report.

DAILY NOTES AND RECORDS

The purpose of this form is to make sure that any procedures which you perform can be accurately recorded and placed with an appropriate date of occurrence. This form can be set up in a number of different formats. You want to create a format that is easy to read and easy to locate specific information.

You will need to write down subluxation levels, listings, adjustment procedures, dates, modalities used, x-ray procedures, examinations, reevaluations, and recommendations which you may make to a patient during an office visit. This form needs to be designed properly so that a doctor can instantly glance down and see what procedures were administered to a patient on a given date.

AUTO ACCIDENT INFORMATION FORM

This form is necessary in order to collect necessary information regarding patients that have been injured in automobile accidents. Information such as date of accident, time of accident, description of incident, police information, impact description, and vehicle questions all need to be recorded here. This form will help the auto accident patient to carefully reconstruct the most important and essential facts of the incident.

WORKER COMPENSATION FORM

A worker's compensation form will help make filing insurance claims that much easier. Information is carefully collected and reported onto this form. Information regarding the nature of the accident, employer, individual authorizing care, treatment performed prior to entering your office should all be captured within this paperwork.

RETURN TO WORK FORM

This form is a written authorization for your patient to return back to work. This type of paperwork is almost always required by the patient's place of employment in order for that individual to be able to legally return back to work. Recommendations for light duty and any other restrictions that need to be observed by the employer are labeled on this document and sent back with the patient to give to an authorized company official.

DOCTOR'S LIEN FORM

This form is designed to allow an attorney to pay off a patient's outstanding doctor bill after the disbursement of a settlement from an insurance company. The doctor bill is paid out of the insurance settlement and then the balance of the award is distributed to the patient. This is commonly used in personal injury cases resulting from automobile accidents.

NARRATIVE REPORT

A narrative report is a lengthy 2-3 page report that describes the history, treatment phase, and future prognosis of a patient that has been under care in your office. These reports are usually requested by an attorney who represents the patient in a lawsuit involving an auto accident or some type of personal injury scenario. These types of reports are then used by the attorney as expert testimony from the treating doctor. The attorney will expect to pay a professional fee for the writing of such narrative reports. The fee for such reports will vary depending on the length and sophistication of the presentation. A fair price range to charge for the preparation of such a document is between $125.00- $350.00.

SIGNATURE ON FILE FORM

A signature on file form is kept in the patient's permanent file. It is a form that is signed once by the patient and it grants permission to the doctor to use that patient signature over and over again in order to execute insurance transactions and other patient related business.

PATIENT ITEMIZED BILLING STATEMENT

Depending on whether or not you have your office billing completed by computer software, you may or may not need to create a billing statement for patients and insurance companies. If you utilize a software program, the creation of such a form is not necessary. For those practitioners that do not utilize modern technology, the creation of such a form is relatively simple and easy to fill out. The form should include the patient's name, address, phone number, dates of service, procedure codes, diagnostic codes, professional fees charged, payment received from patient, and total balance still due to your office. At the bottom of the statement the chiropractor's name, license number, and social security or tax identification number should be listed. It is also important to place the name of your practice along with an address and phone number on this form as well as any of the previous forms that we have been writing about in this chapter.

When you prepare this statement it will be necessary to design the form in a column format and allow room for five or six office visits so that multiple visits can be submitted to insurance companies every month. This type of statement is commonly used in an office where the doctor accepts "assignment of patient benefits" on a regular basis. This means that the doctor performs the professional services and accepts only the applicable co-payment (the portion of the fee which the patient's insurance company will not pay for) from the patient and awaits payment directly from the insurance company.

If you choose not to accept "assignment of patient benefits" you should design a billing statement in the format of which is commonly known as a "super bill" design. This type of statement will allow direct submission of billing to the insurance company via the patient after first paying the doctor directly at the time the services are being rendered.

PATIENT SIGN IN FORMS

Patient sign in forms are an important record of who actually visited your office on a given day. With this document there can be no confusion as to which patients were at your office, and which patients cancelled their appointments. It is our recommendation that all chiropractors have a sign in sheet prepared for each practice day in which they operate.

DISABILITY CERTIFICATE

A disability certificate is a necessary form that you will need to fill out on occasion for patients that have been out of work or for patients that you would like to keep out of work for a period of time. The format is short and to the point and it will indicate whether the patient will be partially or totally disabled and for how long. This form is filled out by the chiropractor and then given to the patient who will in turn present the paper to an employer.

RECORDS TRANSFER FORM

The ability to have a set of records transferred from another office to your own is accomplished by submitting a records transfer form. This document is easily created and grants official permission, with an authorized signature from the patient, for one practitioner to send a copy of the patient's file to a new doctor.

Sample Forms For Your Office

This section includes a collection of office forms that we wrote about in the previous chapter. We have prepared these forms for use in your own office. As we stated earlier in this book, you may feel free to copy them verbatim, modify their content, or alter their appearance entirely. We hope that this will help you get the paper work portion of your office up and running smoothly.

All of these forms can be purchased from a medical supply house or printing company for about a thousand dollars. If you use our forms and copy them on a computer you can generate a master form and take it to a copy store for mass production at a nominal fee.

The order in which you should assemble your office forms for a patient file is listed below:

1. Patient registration information
2. Patient health history
3. Consent to chiropractic care
4. Spinal Examination
5. Radiographic report
6. Daily notes and records
7. Insurance and signature on file forms
8. Patient itemized billing statement
9. Additional forms that need to be added

PATIENT REGISTRATION INFORMATION

Name_____

Date_____

Address_____

Sex_____ Date of Birth_____Marital Status _____

Patient SS #_____ Job Title _____

Company_____

Company Address_____

How did you learn about our office?

_____

Home Phone Number_____Work Number_____

In case of emergency who should we notify? _____

_____

INSURANCE INFORMATION

Name of Insured _____

How are they related to the patient?

_____

Insurance Company_____

Policy #_____

Amount of Deductible _____

Subscriber's Name_____D.O.B._____

Insurance ID#_____

Direct Payment to Doctor / Release of Records: I state that I have insurance with_____ and assign to this office all allowable insurance benefits payable to me for chiropractic services rendered to me (or my dependent). I further understand that regardless of coverage I am ultimately responsible for any charges incurred at this office. I hereby authorize Dr._____ to release all health information in my file to any insurance company or adjuster necessary to process insurance claims for benefits that are payable under the terms of my insurance policy.

Insured's Signature_____

ACCIDENT INFORMATION

Date of Accident_____
How did the Accident occur? _____
Who has been notified about your accident? _____

Have you retained an attorney at law? Yes / No
Name of attorney_____
Address of Attorney _____
Phone Number_____

PATIENT HEALTH HISTORY

Name_____

Date_____

Address_____

_____

What is your complaint today? _____

When did this condition begin? _____

Grade the level of your pain from 1-5 with 1 being the least painful and 5 being the most painful._____

How frequent is the pain you experience? _____

Have you received any treatment for this condition prior to contacting our office? _____

Please list the names of any health care practitioners you have seen for this condition in the spaces listed below:

_____

_____

_____

_____

_____

Do you currently have any health related conditions that our office should be aware of that might be important for us to know about? _____

_____

_____

_____

_____

_____

_____

Have you had any health related conditions, in the past, that our office should be aware of that might be important for us to know about? _____

_____

_____

_____

_____

_____

Please list below any surgical procedures or operations that have been performed on you and please list applicable dates for each individual surgery. _____

_____

_____

_____

_____

_____

_____

_____

Please check any of the following activities you regularly take part in:

Daily exercise () Smoking () Consumption of alcohol () Recreational Drugs () Caffeine products ().

Please list below any medications that you are actively taking and the reason why you are taking such medications.

_____

_____

_____

_____

_____

_____

Patient's Signature _____

Legal Guardian's Signature_____

CONSENT TO CHIROPRACTIC CARE:

When an individual seeks chiropractic healthcare and a practitioner of chiropractic accepts that person as a member of their practice, it is vitally important that both parties have the same desired goals in mind. The objective of chiropractic is to remove a type of nerve interference that can occur from time to time in the human being known as vertebral subluxation.

Vertebral subluxations are tiny misalignments of one or more of the 24 vertebrae in the spinal column. These misalignments can cause an alteration of nerve function which in turn causes a distortion and malfunction to the transmission of mental impulses, resulting in a lessening of the body's innate ability to express its maximum health potential.

A chiropractic adjustment is a specific manual force (done by hand) which helps the body to bring about a correction of the vertebral subluxation. Our method of correction in this office is by administering specific adjustments to the spine for the correction of vertebral subluxations when detected by careful chiropractic examination and analysis.

We do not offer to diagnose or treat any disease or condition other than vertebral subluxation. If during the course of our spinal examination process we happen to find unusual findings that are outside of the scope of our chiropractic practice objective, we will advise you of such findings. If it is your desire to seek advice or more information about such findings such as a diagnosis or treatment we will recommend that you seek the services of a health care provider who specializes in that area.

I, _____

have read and fully understand the above description of chiropractic and the services that will be performed in this office. I therefore undertake chiropractic care on this basis.

Patient Signature_____

Date_____

Legal Guardian's
Signature_____

Date_____

SPINAL EXAMINATION

_____ Initial Exam
_____ Re-evaluation

Name: _____ Date: _____

Head Tilt:	Left	Neutral	Right
Shoulder Height:	Left	Neutral	Right
Hip Height	Left	Neutral	Right

LEG CHECKS:			FINDINGS
Prone Short Leg	Left	Balanced	Right
Pelvic Analysis	LPP	—	RPP
	LPN	—	RPN
Cervical Syndrome	LCS	NCS	RCS
Sacral Analysis	LSR	NSR	RSR
Supine Short Leg	Left	Balanced	Right

RANGE OF MOTION:

Cervical:		
	Flexion / Extension	Normal / Restricted
	L Lateral Flexion	Normal / Restricted
	R Lateral Flexion	Normal / Restricted
	L Rotation	Normal / Restricted
	R Rotation	Normal / Restricted

Thoracic:		
	Flexion / Extension	Normal / Restricted
	L Lateral Flexion	Normal / Restricted
	R Lateral Flexion	Normal / Restricted
	L Rotation	Normal / Restricted
	R Rotation	Normal / Restricted

Lumbar		
	Flexion / Extension	Normal / Restricted
	L Lateral Flexion	Normal / Restricted
	R Lateral Flexion	Normal / Restricted
	L Rotation	Normal / Restricted
	R Rotation	Normal / Restricted

Pelvis: Note Areas of Restricted Motion Below:

_____

_____

PALPATION FINDINGS:

Listings / Comments:

C1_____ C2_____ C3_____ C4 _____ C5_____ C6_____
C7_____
T1_____ T2_____ T3_____ T4_____ T5 _____ T6_____
T7_____ T8_____ T9 _____
T 10 _____ T11_____ T12_____
L1 _____ L2 _____ L3 _____ L4_____ L5 _____ Sacrum_____
Lt. Hip _____ Rt. Hip _____

ORTHOPEDIC / NEUROLOGICAL TESTS:

Lt. Rt. Normal   Abnormal

Bechterew
Allens
Minors
Soto Hall
Adams
Braggard
Milgrams
Nachlas
Yeomans
Trendelenburg's
George's
Patrick Fabere
Fajersztajns
Toe Walk
Heel Walk
Straight Leg Raise
Adson's
Kemp's
Shoulder Depression
Cervical Distraction
Foraminal Compression

REFLEXES:

	Left	Right
Triceps		
Biceps		
Radial		
Brach / Rad		
Patellar		
Achilles		

DERMATOME FINDINGS:

C2___ C3___ C4___ C5___ C6___ C7___ C8___ T1___
L1___ L2___ L3___ L4___ L5___ S1___

Codes: Normal = N
        Hyper   = H+
        Hypo   = H −
        Absent = A

X-RAYS REQUESTED: Cervical Thoracic Lumbar Pelvis

Lateral A-P Flexion Extension Left Oblique Right Oblique
Others

(Additional information can be added or information shown can be deleted based on your philosophical bias.)

RADIOGRAPHIC REPORT

Patient Name _____ Date of Films _____

Examination of
Cervical Spine: Lat () APOM () Obliques () Flexion () Extension

Scoliosis_____

Lordotic Curve _____

Degenerative Changes _____

Other Findings_____

Thoracic Spine   Lateral () AP () Other ()

Scoliosis_____

Kyphotic Curve _____

Degenerative Changes_____

Other Findings _____

Lumbar Spine & Pelvis: Lateral () AP () Other ()

Scoliosis_____

Lordotic Curve_____

Degenerative Changes_____

Other Findings_____

RADIOGRAPHIC LISTINGS:

C1_____

C2_____

C3_____

C4_____

C5_____

C6_____

C7_____

T1_____   T7_____

T2_____   T8_____

T3_____   T9_____

T4_____   T10_____

T5_____   T11_____

T6_____   T12_____

L1_____

L2_____

L3_____

L4_____

L5_____

Sacrum_____   Right Hip_____   Left Hip_____

Chiropractor's Signature_____Date_____

PATIENT DAILY NOTES AND RECORDS

Patient Name_____

Date of Activation_____

Male () Female ()   Date of Birth_____

Insurance () Cash () Family Plan ()

Insurance Company_____

Date:

Subjective:

Objective:

Assessment:

Corrective Procedure:

Plan of Care:

Date:

Subjective:

Objective:

Assessment:

Corrective Procedure:

Plan of Care:

AUTO ACCIDENT INFORMATION

Name_____

Date of Accident_____

Location of Accident_____

Please describe, with as much detail as possible, the nature of the accident. _____

_____

_____

_____

_____

_____

_____

_____

_____

Where were you located in the motor vehicle? _____

_____

_____

_____

What was the total number of passengers in the vehicle?

_____

What were the driving conditions like on the day of the accident?

_____

_____

_____

_____

What speed were you driving at when the accident occurred?

_____

What type of vehicle were you driving? _____

Did you have a seat belt on during the accident? Yes ( ) No ( )

Did you hit another vehicle? Yes ( ) NO ( ) If yes, what type of vehicle did you hit? _____

_____

If your car did not hit another vehicle, what object did you hit?

_____

_____

Did any portion of your body hit a part of the vehicle during the accident? Yes ( ) No ( )

If you checked "Yes" please explain what body parts were involved? _____

_____

_____

_____

_____

Did you report this accident to the Authorities? Yes ( ) No ( )

If yes, please explain. _____

_____

_____

_____

_____

Please describe your condition after the accident.

_____

_____

_____

_____

_____

_____

_____

What type of treatment did you receive after the accident?

_____

_____

_____

_____

_____

_____

_____

_____

What type of x-ray films were taken by doctors regarding your condition? _____

_____

_____

_____

_____

_____

_____

How many work days have you actually missed as a result of this auto accident? _____

_____

_____

Please list any injuries or symptoms that you currently have as a result of this accident.

_____

_____

_____

_____

_____

_____

_____

_____

_____

_____

_____

Do you currently have difficulty performing any activities as a result of this accident? _____

_____

I certify that the information on this form is both accurate and true.

Patient's Signature_____ Date_____

WORKER COMPENSATION INFORMATION

Date _____

Patient Name _____Date of Birth _____

Address_____

_____

Phone Number_____Job Title _____

_____

Company you work for? _____

_____

Company Phone Number_____

Company official in charge of case

_____

Please explain where and when the injury took place. _____

_____

_____

_____

_____

_____

_____

_____

What was the name of the person who you contacted regarding your injury? _____

_____

_____

Have you received any treatment for this condition prior to coming to this office? _____

_____

_____

_____

_____

_____

_____

COMPANY AUTHORIZATION FOR CARE

I, _____ an authorized representative

of_____

_____company

authorize treatment for injuries sustained on the job for

_____. I understand that I am

personally responsible for payment of services that are being

rendered to _____by Dr._____

Care is authorized until the date of_____

Authorized Signature_____

Date_____

RETURN TO WORK INSTRUCTIONS

Name_____

Date_____

Date of accident or injury_____

Analysis: Subluxations at the levels of: C4-C6, T5-T7

Corrections which were rendered to patient: Chiropractic corrective adjustments to the spine.

() Patient cannot return to work at this time. A new exam will be performed on _____

() Patient is able to return to work with the following limitations._____

_____

() Patient is able to return to work with no limitations as of

_____

Any limitations placed on this employee will remain in place until the date of_____

Doctor's Signature _____Date_____

Authorization to Release Patient Information:

I hereby authorize my chiropractor to release any information or copies of my chiropractic office file to my employer or their insurance company. The authorization is valid only for those records that are related to the treatment for injuries which I sustained while on the job working for the _____company.

Patient's Signature _____Date_____

DOCTOR'S LIEN

To: Attorney(s) _____

_____

_____

Patient's Name _____

I hereby authorize and direct you to pay to Dr. _____
_____any
outstanding sums or balances owed to him for professional
services rendered to me by him in association with my accident
on _____. I hereby authorize you to pay Dr.
_____ directly out of the
funds collected as a result of any settlement regarding my
case.

I also understand that in the event that such a settlement is
not made that I am still fully responsible for all chiropractic
fees that may accumulate during my care at Dr. _____
_____office.

I authorize Dr._____ to release any
copies of my chiropractic file to my attorney(s) for their
inspection in order that they can represent me properly in a
legal manner.

Patient's Signature_____Date_____

The undersigned attorney(s) represent the above named patient in this case and hereby agree to observe all of the conditions and terms of this lien, and agree to protect the above named doctor in his or her financial interests regarding this case.

Attorney(s) Signature _____Date_____
Attorney(s) Signature _____Date_____

NARRATIVE REPORT

Mr. Anybody's Attorney, Esq.
1234 Main Street
Anywhere, USA 12345

RE: John Smith
Your File # 11111
Date of Accident: 1/10/99

Dear Mr. Anybody's Attorney:

John Smith presented in my office on January 16, 1999 complaining of severe pain and stiffness in his neck and lower back which was accompanied by frequent headaches. He informed me that he was in an automobile accident on January 10, 1999, in which another vehicle cut out in front of his resulting in a T-bone type collision. He reported that he was in the driver's seat, wearing his seat belt at the time of the collision. No air bag was deployed. He stated that he began to experience these symptoms shortly after the accident. Prior to this accident, he stated he felt fine. This patient had not been treated in this office prior to January 16, 1999.

A thorough chiropractic examination was conducted which consisted of a postural analysis, range of motion study, prone and supine leg length analysis, static and motion palpation analysis. Cervical and Lumbopelvic x-rays were ordered and analyzed. These exams confirmed the presence of several vertebral subluxations throughout the spine.

A vertebral subluxation is a misalignment of a spinal bone which partially occludes the opening of the intervertebral foramen and neural canal. Such occlusion results in spinal cord and nerve root pressure which produces interference and disrupts proper neural function. This may result in localized symptoms as well as systemic dysfunction.

Postural exam results revealed a left head tilt, high right shoulder, high right hip, and forward head posture. Cervical range of motion was restricted in extension, left and right lateral flexion and right rotation. Prone leg check analysis revealed a contracted left leg in extension and flexion. Supine leg check analysis revealed a contracted right leg. Myospasm with pain and tenderness was noted throughout the cervical and lumbar regions. X-rays of the cervical spine revealed a hypolordosis and posterior body displacement of C2 and C5 on George's Line analysis. The C2 body and spinous were right of midline. The C5 spinous was right of C6. The atlantooccipital articulation was longer on the right indicating right laterality of C1. X-rays of the lumbopelvic region revealed a hypolordosis. Posterior body displacement of L3, L4, and L5 on George's Line analysis with lumbar body rotation to the right was noted. A mild decrease in disc space was noted at L5/S1.

A program of conservative chiropractic care was initiated to correct the patients' subluxations. At first, progress was slow. As his care progressed, the patient began to respond favorably making a full recovery. At the time of his release, he was asymptomatic and back to his pre-accident condition. A program of periodic maintenance exams is recommended to ensure continued spinal health and maximum function.

If I may be of any further assistance in this matter, please feel free to contact me.

Sincerely,

Chiropractor

SIGNATURE ON FILE

I permit the use of this form on all my insurance claims and for the release of any information that is necessary to process insurance claims. I also authorize my chiropractor to act on my behalf in acquiring any insurance benefits that may be payable to me under the guidelines of my health insurance policy. It is also my intention to assign all payable benefits associated with my care at this office directly to the chiropractor. I hereby authorize a photocopy of this authorization form to be used in place of the original document. The original document will remain attached as a permanent part of my chiropractic file and will remain in the chiropractor's office.

Name of Patient _____

SS# _____

Signature_____

Date _____

PATIENT ITEMIZED BILLING STATEMENT

Patient Name_____ File #_____

Date   Pro Code   Diag Code   Charge   Payment   Balance
_____

_____
MAKE SURE THAT YOU ALWAYS USE THE MOST UP TO DATE
_____
PROCEDURE AND DIAGNOSTIC CODES THAT ARE AVAILABLE.
_____
THESE ARE SAMPLE CODES ONLY

Pro Codes:
99201- New Patient Visit
99211- Established Visit
97260-Spinal Adjustment

Diag Codes:
839.0-Cervical Subluxation
839.2-Thor   Subluxation
839.4-Lum   Subluxation

Dr. John Doe
SS# 999-99-9999
License # 000000- New York   Balance Due_____

WELCOME TO OUR OFFICE....

Please sign in below so that we may have a record of your attendance at our office.

Date _____

Name   Time checked in

_____

_____

_____

_____

_____

_____

_____

_____

_____

_____

_____

DISABILITY CERTIFICATE

Date_____

_____ has been a patient at my office and was

() Totally Disabled
() Partially Disabled

from the date of _____ up until _____

Additional
Comments:_____

_____

_____

_____

_____

Chiropractor's Signature _____
Date_____

INSURANCE VERIFICATION FORM

Patient Name_____

Insured's Name_____

Insurance ID card #_____

Insurance Group # _____ Policy #_____

Insurance Company Phone Number_____

Is chiropractic care covered on the policy? _____

What is the yearly maximum amount covered? _____

What is the maximum charge per visit allowed? _____

What percentage is paid by the insurance company? _____

What is the yearly deductible per individual? _____

What is the yearly deductible per family? _____

What date does the deductible start over? _____

How much of the yearly deductible has been satisfied to date?

_____

Does the patient require a referral from another doctor in order to have services considered for benefits? _____

Send claims to: _____

RECORDS TRANSFER REQUEST

Date_____

To: _____

Address: _____

City: _____ State_____Zip_____

I grant permission for the transfer of my official health records or copies of such records and request that they be delivered to the address of the health practitioner listed below. I thank you in advance for your cooperation in this matter.

DR. STEVEN L. REIZER
1234 Anywhere Street
Some where, USA 12345

Name of Patient _____

Signature _____Date_____

Advertising Your Practice

Advertising your practice is very important and should certainly be high on the priority list of things to do in order to get up and running with actual patients visiting you for professional services. There are many clever ways to go about advertising a chiropractic office. Some of these concepts will be more expensive than others, while certain avenues may showcase an office location and the services it provides for next to no cost at all. We have been there before and have experienced the good, the bad, and the ridiculous. Some products in advertising may work very well with one profession or trade and not so well in another. This is also the case within the profession of chiropractic.

In this chapter we would like to go over some of the different advertising schemes that will probably cross your path within the first year of opening your practice. We will write about the product and explain how it is supposed to work. Next, we will tell you how it really works in conjunction with the chiropractic profession. With this information at your disposal you will be able to pick and choose very wisely how you spend overhead when trying to advertise your practice.

DIRECT MAIL PACKAGE

Direct mail advertising takes a customized brochure or flyer and sends it directly via the United States Postal Service to thousands of residents in a specific postal zip code. There are many companies specializing in this business and they will usually contact new chiropractic offices as soon as they learn of your location. The fee for this service which includes the design and production of the flyer and the postage to get it out to about ten thousand residents is between $400-$600 dollars a circulation. The advertisement will be placed with other flyers representing other types of businesses. Direct mail companies will usually limit the number of chiropractors in a zip code to just one doctor.

You can expect a very low return on your investment for this type of campaign. About 3-4 responses out of 10,000 would be considered good. Realistically it is not out of the question to get zero responses out of an entire circulation. Most people consider this product "junk mail" and do not even bother to open it up. It goes directly into the garbage along with your flyer. We rate this product very low and suggest you spend your advertising dollars on another product.

NEWSPAPER ADVERTISEMENTS

Newspaper advertisements will showcase your display ad in front of large numbers of subscribers. These types of advertisements can be extremely expensive and the end results are often quite disappointing. In order for newspaper advertising to work it must be done repetitiously in conjunction with a long advertising program. People reading your ad must get in the habit of seeing it every day or at least a couple of times per week. It takes this type of constant bombardment by an advertiser in order to get any type of positive results. Thousands of dollars can be blown on newspaper advertising without seeing any return on your investment. If you happen to practice in a town that has a small community publication, where you can afford to advertise on a regular basis throughout the year, this may be a good product for you to consider. In this situation the results will show favorable statistics. If on the other hand you are going to advertise 10 or 15 times a year in a daily publication, we suggest that you spend your money else where. This kind of sporadic print media advertising will not work that well.

YELLOW PAGES

The *Real Yellow Pages* or the one that is put out by the telephone company that provides your phone service is an important place to have an advertisement. This ad is going to cost big bucks and if you cannot afford to pay for it, the phone company will turn off the phone service to your business. We suggest a minimum size ad or listing in order that prospective patients can locate your name and business number should they have exposure to your office from another source. A small display advertisement in the phone book is not a bad idea. There is a decent return on this product.

You do not need to take out large display advertisements in the *Yellow Pages* as the expense is enormous and the reward is not that great. Many people in the community are also aware of the expensive nature of yellow page advertising and will shy away from offices with large display advertisements. These potential patients may feel that the doctor might have to charge expensive professional fees to pay for the campaign.

You should also be aware of imposters that claim to be the

Yellow Pages and who try to sell you display advertising in a book that will probably never be circulated. These solicitations often are designed to look like an invoice or bill. Do not be fooled, this is a scam and you do not have to send a dime into these people. This is a different publication put out by a company that has nothing to do with your phone service. Throw the invoice invitation away.

RADIO AND TELEVISION

Radio and television advertising will yield very solid results for you provided you sign up for a campaign that is promoted throughout the entire year. Again, this is a product that will absolutely not work if it is done on a sporadic schedule. Usually 30 second commercials are long enough and of course 60 second commercials are twice as good. The advertising rates for radio and television are extremely expensive. This is probably not even a consideration for a practitioner just beginning a new office. The best time for radio advertising is known as "drive time" which is the time of day people are driving to and from work in the early morning and late afternoon.

Television prime time is also early morning before going to work and later in the evening when people are returning home to watch the news or network programming which features a wide variety of sitcom style shows.

This is an option for more established chiropractors looking to maintain or raise the level of their business to a higher degree. Beginners should stay clear from radio and television products.

ADVERTISING SPACE ON BACK OF CASH REGISTER RECEIPTS

When you go to the store and you purchase grocery items you will get a cash register receipt. If you turn that receipt over you will see companies featured on the back of the paper as advertisers. The price to get on this "throw away" piece of paper is $400-$600 or higher for a given period of time. This is not the way people will decide which chiropractic office to visit. Do not fall for this gimmick, as it will produce very minimal results.

SPEAKING ENGAGEMENTS

A speaking engagement at a club or organization in your surrounding community is probably one of the best forms of advertisement a doctor of chiropractic can take part in. This is great exposure for you and your office and it will not cost you a dime. The audience which you target can have direct contact with the doctor and this type of interaction will lead to an influx of new patients.

There are literally hundreds of clubs and organizations in your community that need to fill slots with speakers for their meetings and various functions that they put on throughout the year. These clubs and organizations would be delighted to have a young doctor come in and talk about the tremendous healing capabilities of chiropractic.

Go to your public library and ask the librarian for an index book of all organizations and official clubs that exist within your immediate community. Photocopy the pages and then take a magic marker and work your way down the list of potential groups. You should try to have at least one speaking engagement per month. If you do this on a regular basis you will generate a large number of new patients that will be eager to sign up at your office. This is a must for new doctors just starting out!

BUSINESS CARDS

Business cards, as we stated in an earlier chapter, are probably one of the best advertising products you can purchase. These cards are economical, easy to store, and most importantly very easy to carry around with you at all times. The more you give out, the more visible your practice becomes. Never be shy about giving out business cards to advertise your office. When you go out to dinner always be sure to leave behind your card. Whenever you attend functions of any sort you should leave your business card. Remember that business cards are like seeds in a garden. The more of them you plant the better the chances will be that patient volume will grow in your office.

CALENDARS, PENS, MONTHLY PLANNERS

Items such as calendars, pens, and monthly planners can be given away to patients in order that they have your office name and number handy at all times. The products which you give out will advertise your business to patients all year long as your advertising information is printed onto the items.

This is actually a pretty good idea and it is relatively cheap to participate in this kind of a promotion. This also keeps already established patients thinking of your business on a regular basis. Patients like to get free gifts and they will show them off to friends and other family members. The objective in advertising is to show off your business and to get others to talk about your product. These little gifts and token pieces can help you to accomplish this goal.

PRESS RELEASES

A press release is a written advertisement about you or your office that does not have to be paid for. It will not cost you one cent. Anytime you attend a seminar, add a new service to your practice, have a grand opening party you can submit a press release to the newspapers and have them publish it for free so the community will know every event that occurs regarding your business.

Type up a small summary of what you have accomplished and then submit the paper to the publication you want the release to be featured in. Call the publication on the phone and ask them to give you the fax number for the "Press Release Editor." You can fax your release right from your office to all of the local newspapers in your area. This is absolutely free exposure for your business.

BILL BOARDS AND HIGHWAY SIGNS

Outdoor advertising via the use of billboards on major highways can be an extremely expensive proposition. We simply recommend that you not do this right out of the gate. The results vary depending on what locations your boards are placed at. If you can secure a location for a huge sign close to your office you may actually get some moderate to good results. The problem with this kind of product is that a large sign usually will cost about $1,400 a month to lease. You would have to attract a large number of new patients per month to pay for that expense. This is very risky and should be avoided by new practitioners.

ADVERTISING YOUR OFFICE IN A MOVIE THEATRE

Before the movie house begins showing the actual feature film, there is a period of time that advertisements are flashed up on the screen. Most of this type of display advertising is accomplished by "still shot photography" and not by motion photography. This kind of a program is not going to build your practice over a period of a couple of weeks. If you want to try a campaign such as this it will require a long term commitment on your part. The expense involved with this type of program is moderate to low. It may be a viable source of exposure for you if the proximity of the theatre is reasonably close to your office location.

PHONE SOLICITATIONS FROM POLICE AND FIRE FOUNDATION

A phone call will come into your office and on the line will be someone claiming to be associated with your local police or fire department. The solicitor will ask you to support the organizations by placing an ad in a publication that will be coming out for the benefit of these groups. The advertisement will usually run about $300-$600 for the year and the solicitor will ask you to send in about 10-12 business cards with your payment so the cards can be put up in the local fire station or police department.

This, at first appearance, seems like it might be a pretty good idea. It also seems like a good group of organizations to support within your community. It is pretty hard to say "no" to the policeman or fireman on the phone.

Learn to say *no* to this scam. If you fall for this you will be the target of numerous solicitations with similar copy cat schemes. These people will bleed your bank account dry. They are relentless and you will not get a single patient referral from them. The person who calls you on the phone is not a member of the police or fire department but instead an employee of a company that will put out this advertisement booklet. The company has contacted the police or fire department. They have been authorized to set up the program for these organizations, and in return for being able to run their program they will make a donation to the police or fire house at the conclusion of the program. The donation they make is minuscule compared to the profit they will earn. Copies of the advertisement booklet will be sent out to some of the members of the police and fire squads, but you will not get referrals and the business cards you send in will be collected by the company running the program and placed in a file with your name so they can be sure to call you the following month for another civic minded cause.

When you get this type of call you need to be firm and just as aggressive as the other person that is trying to steal your money. Tell the person that you allocate a certain amount of dollars per year to charitable causes and the amount you have set aside for the current year has already been exhausted. Also explain that you have a direct relationship with the organizations which you choose to support and that their company should take your name off of their list for any future projects they may be working on. Once you make this point clear to these people the solicitation requests will stop.

BE SMART WITH YOUR ADVERTISING DOLLAR

The most important thing to remember is that you need to be smart when spending overhead to promote or advertise your business. Some forms of advertisement will be helpful in promoting the growth of your business while other options will generate no form of measurable response. Track everything that you try and see if it works in the market where you have set up. If something is a winner you fly with it. The minute it stops working you put it on the shelf and try something else. Do not get emotional with advertising, as it is only a tool to help you build your patient base and nothing more. All tools have a price and when they are no longer useful for your trade you need to discard them.

Preparing Year End Tax Records

At the end of the business year you will have to gather and provide financial information about your practice for your accountant. It is very important that you have your information organized in a neat manner so that your year end tax return to the federal government can be prepared by your tax professional accurately.

It would probably be a very good idea to contact an accountant or tax preparer before you begin your practice. A professional tax consultant can explain how to set up a record keeping system for tax purposes right from the very beginning. If you decide not to contact such a professional we suggest that you follow the information in this section very carefully.

PEG BOARD LEDGER

A peg board ledger is a very neat and orderly way to record income that is generated from your practice. A peg board is a vinyl covered board with tiny raised pegs that protrude from the left side. A record sheet with tiny perforations that match the configuration of the pegs is placed and secured on to the board. Each patient that comes into the office is assigned a ledger card and their name and address along with account information is recorded on this card. The cards are then stored in a ledger card tray in alphabetical order. When the patient comes into the office the ledger card is removed from the tray and placed on top of the pegboard record sheet. The date of service, office procedures, charges, payments, and running balance for this patient are all recorded on to this ledger card. The ledger card is a carbon form which also transfers the information on to the record sheet. After the information is recorded the ledger card is filed away in the tray until the next visit needs to be recorded.

At the end of the day or week you will have a neat record of every transaction in your office on one or two record sheets. At the end of each week you simply calculate the amount of income you received and record and circle the number at the bottom of the last sheet. You do not record any charges that are outstanding. Only the payments that have actually come into your office need to be recorded and circled as income earned for that week. At the conclusion of the business tax year you will gather all of your record sheets and add up the totals that you have circled at the end of each week. The grand total will be the gross income generated from your business during that year.

Once you have calculated your gross income it will be necessary for you to calculate any refunds that you have given back to your patients or insurance companies. If you have sent back refunds it is important that you subtract the total number of refunds that you gave back from the total of your gross income. This new calculation will become the new gross income.

TAX DEDUCTION RECORDS

Tax deductions are allowable business expenses that can

legally be subtracted from your total gross income. There are many categories of business tax deductions that are allowable by the Internal Revenue Service. There are also some business expenses that will not be allowable in your calculation. The best thing for a doctor to do is to record all of the expenses he or she may incur during the course of the year and let a professional tax consultant determine what is or is not allowable for that particular tax year. In reality, the tax laws change from year to year. What may be allowable during one business year may not be allowable for the following business year.

In order to record possible business tax deductions it will be necessary for you to categorize each deduction into specific groupings. The best way to approach this is to look at a "Schedule C" Internal Revenue Service form. A "Schedule C" form is where business related income and deductions are recorded for sole proprietors. If you incorporate your business or form a partnership you will need to consult an accountant. Categories for business deductions are listed below:

Rent	Utilities
Phone	Supplies
Vehicles	Insurance
Advertising	Equipment
Travel	Meals
Seminars	Licensing Fees
Uniforms	Laundry
Office Cleaning	Postage
Taxes	Donations

Each category should be placed on a piece of paper and you

should make one sheet of paper for each month of the business year. During the course of each month you should also keep a running record of each business expense which you incur and record it on a sheet of paper as well. At the end of each month, total the amount for each category and indicate that amount on the monthly category page. In addition to this you should get a large envelope to hold each expense receipt that you are given when you pay a bill. Everything from postage receipts to utility bill stubs should be placed into this envelope and stored in a safe location.

At the end of the business year you simply pull out the twelve monthly business expense category sheets and total up your expenses for the year. When you are finished you will know how much you spent in each category. When you walk into your accountant's office you will have the gross income ledger sheets and expenses you have incurred for the entire year neatly divided up into workable categories.

This will make your tax preparer very happy and cause him or her to charge you less money for professional accounting services. If the accountant is required to do all of this additional leg work you can be assured that you will be billed accordingly for the extra service being performed.

It is not necessary for you to bring in any of your tax receipts for the accountant to see. Simply keep them in a safe place in case you ever have to prove that the expenses were actually legitimate. You only need to bring the final calculations to the accountant. From this information a proper tax return can be prepared concerning the operation of your practice. Your accountant will tell you how long you must keep tax records before they can be legally discarded.

We have prepared some sample forms on the following pages to show you how to record these business expense deductions by category.

Tax Deduction Record

Month_____

Date	Item	Amount	Check #	Cash Payment
1-02-01	Rent	$ 700.00	1213	N/A
1-05-01	Electric	$ 134.00	1214	N/A
1-07-01	Phone	$ 127.00	1215	N/A
1-11-01	Supplies	N/A		$ 63.24

Continue to list as above

Monthly Tax Deductions Totaled By Category

Rent	$700.
Utilities	$196.
Phone	$ 127.
Insurance	$ 145.
Supplies	$ 117.
Uniforms	$ 29.
Laundry	$ 14.
Cleaning	$ 110.
Equipment	$ 517.
Postage	$ 43.
Seminars	
Travel	
Meals	
Taxes	
Vehicles	$ 185.
Donations	$ 25.
Misc.	$ 10.

Month: January- 2000

Yearly Tax Deduction Record

Rent
Utilities
Phone
Insurance
Supplies
Uniforms
Laundry
Cleaning
Equipment
Postage
Seminars
Travel
Meals
Taxes
Vehicles
Donations
Miscellaneous

—————————————————>   Totals turned into your accountant.

Patient Management

One of the most important aspects of running a chiropractic office is the ability to manage patients in an organized manner. Up until this point we have discussed, for the most part, preparation requirements that were necessary in order to begin a chiropractic practice. We will now direct our attention to the initial encounter between chiropractor and patient. The business of patient management is an art all by itself and must be mastered by the chiropractor if a successful practice is to be constructed.

TAKING A CASE HISTORY

During the first visit a careful case history should be taken by the chiropractor. It is important here to remember that you are a chiropractor and that you should be gathering information that will help you deliver a chiropractic service. It is also important to remember that chiropractic is a separate and distinct profession from medicine and all of the patient encounters in your office should reflect that. You should include all patient contact information in the history process. (Refer to the forms section of this book to see how this information is requested.) The case history is an interview. The chiropractor is trying to ascertain as much pertinent information from the patient as possible.

One of the items that you hope to learn during this phase of questioning is the reason the patient is seeking your professional services. This one piece of information will allow you to prepare a proper plan of attack for patient education purposes. The type of practice you are operating will determine what type of education actually takes place. Regardless of the philosophical preference of the chiropractor, the patient and the doctor must be on the same page in order for the professional relationship to grow.

During this interview it is important that you also listen very carefully to the patient and their problems. You need to show compassion and concern for a patient. This is not something that you can fake. Be genuine. If you are not concerned about the welfare of the people you see in your office, you should probably think about working in another profession. If you are not able to listen to the patient you cannot expect the patient to listen to you. Let the patient get everything off of their chest during the first visit. This is going to help the patient to be able to concentrate on you when you begin to talk. Remember, the patient will be listening to you for quite a while after the case history has been taken. You want the patient to be a good listener and this will help you to achieve your goal. This does not take as long as you would think either. Be thorough, but be brief. If the patient starts to ramble on about that time in the fifth grade when he or she skinned their knee on the playground, a pointed question from the chiropractor can get the conversation back on track and up to date.

The next objective is to find out if the patient has ever been to another chiropractor. Sometimes you are actually better off if a patient is coming into your office and has never had any previous exposure to the profession. An individual that has no preconceived notions about your objectives is a blessing in disguise. The patient that has gone to "Dr. Smith" down the road will sometimes compare everything you do and say to that previous professional relationship. If this is the case, you will have your work cut out for you trying to convert the individual over to your line of reasoning. When the proper time presents itself, you explain to the patient that you have a specific objective in mind for their care and that every doctor works a little bit different in their approach to helping a patient. Dialogue such as this will help you to gain the patient's confidence. Make sure that you never say anything of a negative nature about a previous doctor. This is extremely unprofessional and it is a sure way to irritate the patient.

Make sure that you cover and document any injuries, surgeries, fractures, and accidents that the patient might have had in the past. You want to be able to determine if there are any reasons that modification of technique or even the omission of care should be considered. Granted, this is a rare occurrence but there are situations that will present themselves during your practice experience which will fall into this category. If a prior condition is reported to you and it is innocuous in nature you may just want to list the event and the date which it took place. If you feel that a prior condition may play a part as an obstacle in the current level of care you should (OPQRST) the condition in the patient file.

It is also important to have an updated record of medications that a patient is taking. This is not really a part of chiropractic; however should a patient have an adverse reaction to a drug while in your office you may be able to assist a health professional with vital information in the attempt to save a life.

It is important to find out the x-ray history of a patient as well. Although the use of x-rays is an excellent tool for diagnostic and analytical purposes, they are a detrimental force imposed on the human body. The risk to any given patient is extremely minimal with the use of today's sophisticated equipment. Never the less the taking of x-rays have a cumulative effect on a patient and their health.

We both feel that the use of x-rays are certainly warranted in chiropractic care, however we also feel that proper judgment should be utilized when making a decision that will ultimately have an effect on a patient's well being. Someone that has had a tremendous amount of exposure to radiation should probably be put into a program of care with minimal films taken and perhaps analysis can be completed with more palpation (hands on) techniques. Use some good old fashion common sense to come to the right conclusion for your patient.

There are so many important things to ask a patient about their health related history. Most importantly we need to ask chiropractic questions. What physical, chemical, and emotional stresses does the person have to try and adapt to? These are ultimately the "little buggers" that will cause vertebral subluxations to occur. Spend some time trying to acquire this information. Everyone has to face these challenges and it will present an excellent opportunity for you and your patient to begin the education process about how this affects their health and how chiropractic may help.

CONSENT TO CARE / TERMS OF ACCEPTANCE

Another important piece of business that needs to be taken care of during the initial visit is the signing of the *Consent to Chiropractic Care* or *Terms of Acceptance* document by the patient. This form should clearly explain your professional objective. The patient needs to read, understand, and execute written authorization on the document before you actually begin to render any professional services. In addition, a patient that is a minor should have a parent or legal guardian sign the document on their behalf.

This agreement is a written communication inside of the professional doctor / patient relationship that plainly states the chiropractor's intention to provide care to the patient. The legal protection that is provided to the chiropractor from this piece of paper is enormous. A copy of this form should be given to the patient and a copy should be retained inside of the permanent patient file which will remain inside of your office.

NEW PATIENT ORIENTATION

The new patient orientation (NPO) is also given during the first patient visit. This is not the full blown 30 minute presentation that you will give in a group setting inside of your office. This is a 3-5 minute one on one presentation that represents your first attempt at educating the patient. You will explain, in this session, what you will be looking for, **subluxation**. You will also explain to the patient why you are looking for subluxation. The use of a plastic model spine is necessary. You will want to demonstrate a basic anatomy lesson to the patient. Explain how the spine acts as a protective shield to the delicate nervous system and how the individual spinal bones help to form openings for the spinal nerves to pass through. Continue the presentation by explaining the problems that are brought about from misalignment of those spinal bones in relationship to the nervous system. Do not be afraid to illustrate these points with the model spine. Let the patient place their finger inside of the intervertebral foramina as you manipulate the spinal bone in and out of a subluxated state. This is a great teaching method. As the patient feels the opening and closing of the IVF on their finger, a permanent image is being formed in their mind. From this point on, the patient will have a basic understanding of the mechanics associated with subluxation.

You will need to practice the presentation of the short (NPO) over and over again. This is extremely important and you should be able to deliver the performance in its entirety within a five minute period of time. Practice this in front of your spouse, brother, sister, or anyone else that is willing to listen to you. If you have no volunteers for your practice sessions you should practice in front of a mirror. We also recommend that you tape the presentation on audio and video cassette so that you can play it back to hear and see how convincing you are. This short talk needs to be very basic and to the point. Avoid using large and intimidating medical terms. The use of the word **subluxation** is a must.

THE INITIAL EXAMINATION

When performing the initial spinal examination it is important to keep in mind the objective of the exam process. You are gathering physical information to determine if subluxations are present. Make sure that you perform a chiropractic exam! This examination might include a postural analysis, range of motion study, leg checks, instrumentation, and a palpation study. Explain to the patient what you are doing and also why you are doing it. This is another ideal moment to educate the patient.

A postural examination can range from a simple visual analysis to a sophisticated computer aided analysis. The great thing about using a spinal analysis machine or a computer aided analysis is that the patient can step back and look at the distortions in their posture. You can then explain to the patient, with a visual picture in front of the person, that this condition may very well be the result of subluxations in their spinal column. This is what we refer to as "high impact learning." "A picture is worth a thousand words." We are sure you have heard that line before. In reality, this is a very accurate statement. A visual representation of a problem demonstrated properly to the patient is the best form of education on the market.

A range of motion study will assist the chiropractor in determining which areas of the spine are moving freely or are restricted. It is a great way to explain to the patient how subluxations can decrease proper motion of a segment or an entire region of the spine. Remember to constantly educate the patient as you perform the various portions of the study.

As you perform the "leg checks" portion of the exam, make sure you tell your patient how this procedure helps you to isolate the subluxation location in their body or how it helps to establish a pattern. This becomes a continuous process of patient education. The more learning a patient can achieve during your first encounter, the easier the overall education process of that patient will be.

Instrumentation, which is often used in pattern work, can assist the chiropractor in determining when an adjustment may or may not be necessary.

A palpation study is probably the most important part of the chiropractic examination. Explain what you are doing while you are doing it. Keep in mind that a patient may be nervous. You must be confident, reassuring, and professional at all times.

SCHEDULE PATIENT FOR X-RAYS

The next step of this process is to schedule your patient for x-rays. If you decide against the taking of films for your patients you will skip this section and move onto the next area of discussion.

The decision to utilize or not to utilize x-rays may be based on technique or personal philosophy. For example, many doctors have a difficult time justifying the accuracy of looking at a static picture of a dynamic structure such as the spine. When we take a picture of the spinal column or a region of the spine, we are freezing it into a fixed position. It can no longer adapt to its environment like the real spinal column can. When we perform a visual or line analysis on the picture we are sometimes bothered with the idea that spinal listings detected on the film cannot change. We are aware that the subluxations in the patient may change due to the dynamic and adaptive nature of the living person and therefore a professional quandary is often established. Many doctors, however feel perfectly comfortable with looking at static pictures for analysis.

We can all agree, for the most part, that x-rays are very useful in showing degenerative conditions within the spine. They are also very useful in placing patients in a particular phase of degeneration which further establishes the need for chiropractic care. Radiographs can also help us to make a decision as to whether or not it is safe to make an adjustment on a patient. Also we must not discount the fact that a picture of degeneration which is displayed to the patient is a great motivator to that individual to get serious about getting under care. Taking all of this information into consideration it is our suggestion that you schedule your patients for x-rays at this point. Our recommendation is to take full spine films of the cervical, thoracic, and lumbopelvic regions.

FIRST VISIT ADJUSTMENTS

The decision to adjust or not to adjust on the first visit is "yes" or "no" depending on who you talk to in the profession. Those doctors who x-ray patients outside of their office utilizing a radiologist most likely do not adjust on the first visit. Doctors who perform x-ray services in house and those doctors who do not x-ray at all have to decide whether or not to adjust on that first visit.

Our recommendation is not to adjust on the first visit and to make sure that you never let the patient coerce you into such a decision. You must resist the very strong temptation to let the patient call the shots. Remember, you are the doctor and if a patient will not allow you the time to collect and analyze all pertinent information regarding their case, do not accept that patient in your office.

We feel that you should not begin to render care until you have had the opportunity to carefully write a *Plan of Care* (POC) for a patient. This cannot be done until all exam results have been carefully examined and synthesized together. Once the plan of care has been written you will meet with the patient and discuss that plan in the office setting. This period of time when the chiropractor and patient meet to go over the plan of care is known as the *Report of Findings* (ROF) and we will cover both of these topics in great detail next.

REPORT OF FINDINGS

When you meet with your patient for the report of findings, be prepared. Have all x-rays analyzed and marked. Have the results of all exam findings ready. If you plan to use a model spine in your report have that ready as well. Nothing turns a patient off more than a doctor who is unprepared, fumbling around the office looking for things, or making up the presentation along the way. This more than ever is the time to show your patient that you are in control, that you have studied their case, that you have given every finding careful consideration, and you are confident in the recommendations you are about to make.

Next, you simply tell the patient what you have found. Do not try to impress a patient with fancy terminology. Never try to oversell their condition, and conversely, do not undersell a problem. Do not try to make a patient feel bad for failing to see you sooner. Just be honest. Your dialogue might go something like this. "Mrs. Jones, I have the results of all of your exams and I have analyzed your x-rays. I have found four subluxations in your spine and I would like to show you where they are and what it will take to correct them."

Then you would proceed to show the patient their x-rays. Point out on the film where you see evidence of misalignment, any degenerative changes, abnormal findings, etc. It is a good idea to either compare their x-rays with an almost "normal" set or a chart of the phases of degeneration. This can help the patient understand how long their subluxations may have been present. If appropriate, relate what you see on their films with some of your other exam findings (posture, range of motion, palpation, etc.) and/or the patient's reason for seeking care in the first place.

Next, you must answer a patient's most important question, "Can you help me?" The straight chiropractor truly has an advantage here. Because of the objective of the straight chiropractor, (to locate, analyze, and correct subluxations so that the body can better express its inborn ability to be healthy) the answer is always "yes." We are not going to try and persuade you to practice one way over another. You should answer this question honestly. If you feel the service you have to offer will benefit a patient, you must tell the patient so and you must tell the patient how the service will help.

Now that you have told the patient what is wrong and whether or not you can help, you are ready to reveal the Plan of Care you have outlined. The Plan of Care is a natural extension of your Report of Findings.

PLAN OF CARE

After you have analyzed all exam findings, you will want to write up a Plan of Care (POC.) A good POC should provide an outline for you and the patient with regards to the number and frequency of visits and adjustments the patient will need. Several factors may influence these choices such as the patient's condition, phase of degeneration, age, patient's occupation, doctor's technique, and previous chiropractic care.

Some doctors will simply fall into the 3-2-1 trap when it comes to a POC. In other words, they will tell the patient to come in 3 times a week for the first month, 2 times a week for the second month and 1 time a week for the third month. Every patient that comes in will get the same recommendation. Keep in mind that patients will talk. Sometimes patients will talk to each other, especially in your office. Some of them may begin to wonder why their 10 year old who is just coming in for wellness care was given the same POC as the 49 year old patient who was in the automobile accident. Take the time to individualize your POC recommendations.

Use the POC as a guideline, sort of like a roadmap that will take patients from where they are now to a level of maximum improvement and ultimately on into wellness care if they choose to continue. (Remember, it is their choice whether or not they continue. Even though we would like them to, we must allow patients to make that decision on their own while we remain confident in the quality of care and the education we have provided along the way.)

At the conclusion of your Report of Findings and Plan of Care presentation, you can address any questions the patient may have (if you have done a good job, there will be no questions.) Now you need to ask the patient if he or she will accept your recommendations and would like to begin care. Again, let the patient make this decision independently. You cannot force a person to get under care. If the patient decides to go home and think about it, say okay, and let the patient have the necessary time. Resist the urge to push here. You will only come across like you are trying to sell the patient. You will be perceived as needing the patient more than the patient needs you and at that point, you have lost control of the relationship. Respect a patient's decision, be polite and professional, and tell the patient that when the time is right in their mind to start care to give you a call. Patients, in general, will respect you more for not badgering them or trying to coerce them into care and more often than not will call you back to begin care under your terms.

If a patient indicates that he or she accepts your recommendations and is ready to begin care, you will have to answer their second most important question, "How much will it cost?" A simple, straight forward explanation of your office financial policy including your fee structure should be agreed upon before ever accepting or adjusting the patient. We will focus on finances next.

FINANCES

There are a number of ways to handle the financial aspects of running a chiropractic practice. These range from having an all cash practice to having an all insurance practice to anywhere in between. We will begin by examining the most common forms of the cash practice.

CASH PRACTICES

The first type of all cash practice is called an *Honor Fee System*. This is also known as a *Cooperative Fee System* or more commonly as a *Box on the Wall System*. With this arrangement, each patient or family pays whatever they can afford. The patient is responsible for setting their own fee.

Payments are placed into a collection box either on each visit or once each week. A referral component is usually included as part of the patient's fee. In other words, the patient is expected to refer other patients into the office along with depositing their monetary portion into the collection box. Very little record keeping is necessary on the part of the chiropractor and there are no insurance claims or reports to file. You also do not have to wait to get paid. An exceptional patient education program along with a strict set of rules is required for this system to work effectively. Patients must understand that they are expected to come in for care regularly, pay regularly and refer regularly. This system also requires the chiropractor to see a large volume of patients to make up for the lesser fees which patients generally set for themselves.

The next type of cash practice is called a *Fee for Service Practice.* With this system, the doctor sets the fee and the patient pays that fee on each visit. Again, minimal record keeping is required and the doctor gets paid immediately. If you choose this type of fee system, you should set a fee that you are comfortable with and that seems reasonable for the area in which you practice. Payments can be in the form of cash, checks, or credit cards. We both highly recommend that you accept all major credit cards in your practice. This gives your patient an option when cash on hand or in their checking account is low. This is a win-win situation for you and the patient because you still get paid immediately (or within a day or two through electronic transfers) and the patient can receive care immediately and spread their payments out over time if necessary.

Another very popular type of cash practice is to use *Monthly Payment Plans.* This type of fee system goes by several different names as well. It has been called *Family Plans, Unlimited Care at Fixed Fees* (UCAFF), or *Wellness Adjustment Plans*. With these types of plans, the doctor collects a payment once each month for all of the patient's care. We recommend that you have your patients prepay you for the entire month of care. This prevents you from being placed in the position of having delivered a month's worth of care and then having to try and collect from a patient who may not return additional fees. There is minimal record keeping required with these plans however the patient may drop out of care after a month or two (or as soon as their symptom goes away) and you will not have collected as much from the patient as you would in a Fee for Service plan.

When setting your fees, make sure that the fee is both affordable for the patient *and* profitable for you. As an example: If you are charging $50 a month for a husband and wife and they are coming in twice a week, you are only making $3.13 per adjustment. Can you live on that? If you are planning on charging fees like that, you are going to have to make up the difference on volume.

Inevitably, even in the cash practice, you are going to run into the patient who has insurance and you are going to have to decide how to handle this individual. You can simply tell the patient that you do not accept insurance and leave it at that. The patient will probably turn around, walk out of your office, and go to the chiropractor down the street. Another way you could handle this situation is to explain to the patient that you do not accept insurance on assignment and that you require that your patients pay you directly but that you will gladly assist them in filing their bills so their insurance company can reimburse them. You can then provide patients with a receipt or super bill for each visit that lists all of the appropriate insurance codes. There is a bit more record keeping involved here and you will need to familiarize yourself with the insurance codes that match the services you perform. However, many patients will agree to this type of arrangement as it is becoming more and more common even in medical offices where managed care has hurt this practice as well.

INSURANCE PRACTICES

In an insurance practice, the insurance company will be paying for the care of your patient. The insurance company is considered the third party to the traditional doctor patient relationship. When you step into the world of the third party pay system, be prepared to work harder to get paid. Very accurate record keeping is required so that you can track which claims you have sent out and which claims have been paid. You will also be asked from time to time to write a report supplying the insurance company with additional information before they decide whether or not they are going to pay your claim. There is no question that the amount of paperwork will increase, you will wait longer to get paid, and you will spend more time on the phone when you begin dealing with insurance. However, an insurance practice can be very profitable; so many doctors will take on the increased workload. The following information will show you the basics and will enable you to begin accepting insurance from your very first day in practice.

The first thing you will want to do when a patient hands

you their insurance card is to verify if that patient has coverage. We recommend that you make a photocopy of the front and back of their insurance card and keep it in the patient file. Next, call the number on the card to verify their coverage. If there is a toll free number listed, use that, which will save you the cost of the call. There are a number of questions you will want answers to when verifying a patient's coverage. We have created a form for you to follow that has been included in the "forms" section of this book. Sometimes you can find out all of the information from the voice response message by just following the prompts. It is always a good practice to actually speak to a customer service representative however. You will want to find out about their effective date of coverage, deductible amount and if any portion of the deductible has been met to date. You will also want to determine the percentage that the insurance company will pay, co-pay amount, visit or dollar limitations, if the insurance company will send payment directly to the doctor and a claim submission mailing address.

If benefits have been verified, the next thing you should do is to have the patient sign an *Assignment of Benefits* form. This is a form that states that the patient is instructing the insurance company to pay the doctor directly. The patient is assigning their benefits directly to the doctor. As the doctor, you would be accepting assignment. It should also state that the patient understands that he or she is financially responsible for any unpaid balance. You should explain to the patient that he or she is also expected to pay for any service that their insurance company does not cover. Once the Assignment of Benefits is executed, make a copy for the patient and keep the original in their file.

We strongly recommend that you collect all deductible and co-payment amounts, which the insurance company is not responsible for, directly from the patient at the time the services are performed. Remember that co-payments and deductibles are a portion of your fee and you are entitled to collect them. Just because this portion of the professional fee is not paid by the insurance company does not mean that you should let the patient off the hook and not be responsible for the charges.

Very accurate record keeping is a must when dealing with an insurance practice. Every procedure being performed must be recorded and accounted for in the patient file. You should make sure that these records are very neat and legible in case an insurance company requests photo copies of such records. The type of procedure performed and the date of the visit on which a procedure took place should always match the itemized bill and insurance codes which you submit to an insurance company.

The creation of an insurance log is an absolute necessity. An insurance log is simply a record of all insurance claims that have been submitted to insurance companies for consideration of payment. The name of the company, patient, the date which the claim was submitted, and the amount of the claim should be recorded in the log. When the payment of the claim is received or denied the corresponding information in the insurance log should be updated or removed. By having an accurate and updated insurance log a chiropractor can monitor the progress of pending claims. Without a proper insurance log it is difficult to determine the status of a large number of claims. Due to the nature of insurance companies and their inability to process claims in a timely manner, this is a very important tool to construct. An insurance log can be simple or complicated depending on your own preference. It can be placed on a computer file and updated electronically or you can simply write down the information in a notebook pad. Whichever choice you decide on will enable you to track money due to you in an efficient manner.

The actual filing of an insurance claim is not a difficult process. If you choose to file your insurance claims by electronic means there are software packages that you can purchase that will allow you to do this via computer. Most insurance companies will allow you to submit claims either electronically or in hard copy format by mail.

Mail submissions are still the most popular way claims are sent out to insurance companies by chiropractors. A properly filled out itemized bill is attached to either a generic HCFA-1500 insurance claim form or a specific insurance company claim form. All sections of the claim form must be filled in with proper information. Patient insurance policy numbers, group numbers, address, procedure and diagnostic codes, and any other information requested must be filled out on the claim form. A valid patient signature and a valid policy holder's signature must be executed on the form as well. Send the two documents to the proper address indicated on the form or on the patient's insurance identification card and wait for about three weeks for a payment. It is also a good idea to photo copy the claim before you send it off in the mail. On the copy, write down the date which the claim was submitted and circle it in red. Leave the copy in the back of the patient's file. Record the submission date inside of the insurance log which you have already constructed.

The actual insurance codes which you will need to place on

the insurance form and the patient itemized bill can be found inside of a "chiropractic code book" which is published each year with all of the updated procedure and diagnostic codes. There are a number of these publications which are available and they can be purchased for a nominal fee. State licensing boards or a chiropractic state organization can help you get a hold of such information. There are numerous companies that print medical and chiropractic office supplies and they will send you their catalogues in the mail. Chiropractic code books can be purchased from such companies.

Be prepared to follow up on your claim submissions by phone. One or two out of every five claims that you submit will probably need to have some additional follow up on your part. Insurance companies will purposely delay the payment of claims in order to keep money in their accounts to accumulate interest. Just by delaying a claim for a two week period of time can sometimes make an insurance company five or ten dollars. If you multiply this amount by millions of claims that are processed during the course of the year you can imagine the amount of money that is generated by earned interest for that company. We have talked to people in the insurance industry over the years and they have told us on more than one occasion that this is a common practice amongst all insurance companies.

You will also need to be prepared to send out additional information that the insurance company might request. Do not get frustrated and do not lose your cool. Again, this is an attempt to make additional interest for the insurance company. The best thing to do is to submit the information that they are requesting. Eventually you will get paid.

On occasion your claim will be denied and you will have to

submit a written appeal to the company. Send off the appeal and wait to see what type of response you will get. In many instances, a written appeal will get you paid and in certain situations you may not be able to reverse the decision. This is the way that the insurance industry works. If an appeal cannot be reversed it will be necessary to collect your fee from the patient. Remember, the patient is ultimately the individual who is responsible for making sure that the account is satisfied in full regardless of the amount of insurance benefits that may or may not be paid.

One other optional service that some practices may utilize is a claim filing service. This type of service is offered by companies that will submit your billing to insurance companies without you getting involved in the process. The company will handle all of the paper work associated with filing the claims and you will pay them a fee for the service. This is often an attractive product for doctors who do not want to engage in the stress of fighting with insurance companies but still want to offer their patients "assignment of benefits" availability.

Many chiropractors often decide not to accept assignment of benefits because they do not want to get stuck in the middle of a fight between a patient and the patient's insurance company. In this scenario the patient will pay the chiropractor directly for the services being performed and the doctor will file the claim for the patient and instruct the insurance company to reimburse their customer directly. It is still important to keep accurate records of everything going on and an insurance log is still a good idea. The advantage in this situation is that all of the fees are collected right up front. There is absolutely no waiting for your money.

Many practices will often use a combination of these financial strategies within their practice. You will need to think over in your own mind which of these will suit your practice the best. Keep in mind that the system that you choose to create should be easily managed and promote the greatest possibility for you to get reimbursed in the fastest amount of time. This will ultimately create the best possibility for a healthy practice.

Patient Education

Nothing will be more important in the life of your practice than your patient education program. Whatever your definition of success is, most people would agree that a successful practice is one in which the patients return for care on a regular basis. It is also safe to say that most doctors are looking for patients that will pay, stay, and refer others to the practice. When you are getting your patients to do all three of those things, you are truly on your way to a successful practice. The effectiveness of your patient education program is where it all begins.

There are other skills that are necessary to run a practice as well. Your ability to deliver competent, high quality care is extremely important. But in the long run, your success will be measured by how well you educate your patients. There are many doctors who have the ability to generate large numbers of new patients. They have discovered the secret, or they have stumbled onto a foolproof marketing plan that brings in new patients by the bus load. But, many of these same doctors have never mastered the skill of educating their patients. They are constantly dependent on a steady stream of new patients to keep the practice going. This is a very stressful way to practice and unfortunately, for a lot of doctors, leads to burn out.

There are also many doctors who are master technicians. Their ability to deliver high quality care is unmatched. However, many of these doctors are struggling in practice because they too have failed to master the skill of educating their patients. Conversely, there are doctors that are practicing today that are not as accomplished in their technique or perhaps are not quite as successful at attracting tons of new patients but are still doing very well in practice simply because they have learned how to educate their patients properly. Their practice is not dependent on a continuous buffet of new patients because the patients they acquire do not leave. We recommend that you get very good in all three of these areas. The ability to attract new patients, deliver the highest quality of care possible, and mastering the skill of educating your patients will be extremely important to your success as a practitioner.

Rule number one is that you can never educate enough. You should be looking for ways to educate your patients on each encounter that you have with them, keeping your eyes and ears open for that teachable moment. At the same time, you do not want to come across as being overbearing. You will need to utilize good judgment here so you will know when it is time to back off or time to teach. What you should be aiming to accomplish with a patient education program is to reposition chiropractic in the patient's mind. You want to move patients away from thinking of chiropractic as a treatment for back pain and headaches and toward a direction of thinking about chiropractic as a lifestyle of wellness care that respects the inborn wisdom of the body and its use of the nervous system as a tool to achieve optimum health. This next section will address a few of the better ideas that you should include in your patient education program. Keep in mind however, that a good dose of creativity will certainly come in handy here. Do not limit yourself to just the ideas presented in this book.

THE HEALTH TALK

We highly recommend that all of your patients receive a formal health talk. This is by far one of the best tools you can use to educate your patients. It is one of the only opportunities that you will get where your patients are there solely to listen to you talk. Take advantage of this. Whether you call it a health talk, lay-lecture, workshop, new patient orientation, or whatever, you should get into the habit of performing these presentations. This is where you will tell the chiropractic story. The more of these talks that you do, the more comfortable you will become with them. The formal health talk should be done in your office, after hours. It should be a mandatory requirement for all new patients. It is also a good idea to have your patient bring their spouse or a guest to the health talk. Many chiropractors avoid doing health talks because they claim they cannot get their patients to attend. This problem can be overcome simply by scheduling the patient's health talk just as you would schedule one of their adjustments. The dialogue would go something like this. "Mrs. Jones, all of our new patients are required to attend our new patient orientation. It's right here in the office and it usually takes about a half hour. Our next one will be on Tuesday evening at 7:00. I'll schedule your next adjustment for Tuesday at 6:45 so you can attend the orientation right after your office visit. I would also like you to bring your husband or a guest with you."

Occasionally, patients will have a true conflict and for whatever reason their schedule will not allow them to attend your talk. This brings up the question of how often you should offer your health talks. Some doctors perform them every week while others prefer to do one per month. In the beginning, we recommend that you do them every time you get a new patient. Schedule talks even if you only have one new patient attending. These talks are that important. As your practice begins to grow and you start getting more new patients, you can schedule your talks further apart if you wish. We recommend doing at least two talks per month. Under no circumstances should a patient be under care for longer than a month without having attended your health talk. The scheduling conflict can be dealt with in two ways. Primarily, you could offer your talk at another time during the week. For instance, you could perform your health talks on Tuesday evenings and offer a make-up on Saturday mornings. Anyone that could not attend the evening talk could be scheduled for the Saturday morning presentation. Actually schedule these patients in your appointment book for the make-up session and perform the talk just as you would for the evening audience. It does not matter if there is only one patient attending your talk. Do the presentation. Every patient needs to hear the information that you will be speaking about. You will find that the patients that have attended your talk will be better patients. A second way to overcome a scheduling conflict is to have your health talk recorded on video or audio tape. Have a couple of these recordings on hand and if a patient cannot make either of your live talks, send the patient home with a tape. Granted, this is not a preferred approach because there is no guarantee that the patient will actually listen to or watch your tape, however, it is better than just excusing the patient from the education process completely.

PRE-RECORDED HEALTH TALKS

There are pros and cons to using pre-recorded health talks in either the audio or video format. Number one, as we have already mentioned, there is no guarantee that the patient will listen to or watch the tape. You can easily test a patient by having him or her answer a short questionnaire about the talk on their next visit to your office. This is actually quite easy to do. Simply make up a brief quiz that covers the main topics of your talk. Ten questions should be sufficient. Tell patients when you hand them the tapes that they will be required to fill out a brief questionnaire before their next visit so that you can assess their comprehension level of the material. Tell them that this will help you to address any problem areas that they may have. This accomplishes two things. First, it will let you know if they have heard your health talk, and secondly, it gets the point across that you are very serious about the information being presented. This lets the patients know that your talk is not something to be taken lightly or casually. Instead, they will regard your presentation as an important part of their care and since they cannot be there to witness it live, you are making sure that they not only hear it but understand it as well. This can be a very powerful statement. If a patient hands you back a questionnaire with a bunch of wrong answers, you can schedule a time to sit down with this individual and go over the concepts you want the patient to grasp.

There are a number of advantages to using audio over video. First, it is cheaper to produce audio presentations. You can make a very good sounding audio tape right in your home or office. You do not need a bunch of fancy equipment and you do not have to hire someone to record the session. As long as the tape is clear sounding and free of a lot of background noise (dogs barking, kids yelling, phones ringing, etc.) it will be fine. Believe us when we tell you that we have both purchased audio tapes from some of the professions so called leaders only to be sorely disappointed at the quality of the recording. Do not be afraid to record your own tape. Print up a nice looking label either on a home computer or typewriter and you are set. Plan on having about fifteen copies of your presentation available at all times so that you can pass them out as needed. Almost everyone has access to a cassette player. Most people will play the tapes in their car on the way home from your office. Another advantage of audio tape is that patients can listen to the production more than once. They can give the tape to friends, family members and have them listen to your health talk as well. Remember, the more people that hear your health talk, the better.

Video presentations have some advantages also. Some patients are actually more likely to watch videos than listen to audio tapes. Chances are good that a spouse may watch the performance as well. This is a good thing. With video, you can show graphics, flip charts, posters, slides, or some other type of visual aid. When you use video you can also incorporate all of the visual graphics and charts into the presentation for maximum effect and learning. This can make the video presentation almost as good as a live health talk in your office setting. This can be a more expensive route depending on how creative you want to get and how technologically versed you are. This can still be accomplished however, for a relatively small investment by having a friend videotape your live talk.

Whichever method you choose does not really matter. What

is important is that your patients hear and understand your talk. This will lay the ground work for the rest of your patient education program. Another option you should consider is to make both video and audio formats available for distribution to your patients. They are excellent marketing tools to give out. Donating a few copies of your presentation to your local library as a community education service is also a good idea. Of course, you should announce your generous donation with a press release. Get creative!

NEWSLETTERS

One of our all time favorite patient education tools is a newsletter. When you create and publish your own newsletter, you literally create a forum to talk about anything you want. One of the main reasons we like newsletters is that it allows you to reach your patients in their homes on a regular basis. Not only do you get a chance to educate with your newsletter, but you also will be running a very effective marketing program as well by reaching your patients at home. This will keep your name, office, and chiropractic in front of patients and on their minds even when they are not in your office.

The timing of your newsletter is extremely important. We recommend a monthly publication. Other consultants may endorse bi-monthly or quarterly circulation but we strongly disagree. When your practice is young and you are looking for growth, you want to reach your patients as often as possible. The monthly newsletter is one of the best ways to accomplish this. Commit to this project right now, but beware. Once you start doing a newsletter you must keep producing it every month.

This is not an effective tool if it is done haphazardly and at irregular intervals. However, when your newsletter arrives at the first of the month, every month, patients will begin to take notice. They will start to anticipate its arrival. Patients that may not have been in for a few weeks will suddenly show up at your door saying, "I got your newsletter." You may only get to spend anywhere from five to fifteen minutes a week with a patient in your office. A newsletter gives you the opportunity to spend additional time with that patient outside of your office.

What should you write about in your newsletters? Anything you want! Keep it chiropractic, of course. This is your forum, your soap box. Use this opportunity to educate your entire practice about any topic in chiropractic that you desire. For example, you might want to use an article to explain some of the terminology that we commonly use in the profession. You might want to teach about Innate Intelligence. Write an article about symptoms as indicators of health status. You can talk about the need for regular care and about the causes of subluxation. Elaborate on the phases of subluxation degeneration. Break down each section of your health talk and expand them into a series of articles. At least one article of your newsletter should be purely educational. Other topics you can write about include patient testimonials, happenings in your office (in office promotions), healthy living tips, healthy recipes, etc. Use your imagination and be creative. The possibilities are endless.

A newsletter is a very inexpensive way to educate your patients. You do not need a fancy, four page product with glossy paper and accompanying photographs to send out an effective newsletter. A simple one page, 8 ½" x 11" paper printed on both sides can be quite effective. Almost any desktop publishing software will have newsletter templates that you can follow in order to create your own personal publication. Pick a design and a look for your newsletter and get started. Give your newsletter a catchy title and be sure that all of your office contact information is included as well. After you have written your newsletter, you will only need to print one master copy. Take the master copy to any office supply store and for about two cents per copy you can print as many as you need. Stick the newsletters in envelopes and get them in the mail. It is just that simple.

Another good idea is to print extra copies of your newsletter beyond the number which you will mail out. Keep the extras on hand in your office for patients to take home so they can give them out to their friends. Take additional copies and drop them off at a local gym or health food store which you frequent on a regular basis. You should also include a monthly calendar with each newsletter that informs patients of office closings, holidays, in office promotions, etc. Sure, this is an extra page of paper to print each month but most patients will take the calendar with your office name, office hours, and office contact information and stick it on their refrigerator every month. Talk about being in a patient's face all month long! This piece of paper is well worth the extra expense.

BROCHURES, POSTERS & MODELS

Some other very useful patient education materials that you will want to have in your office are brochures, posters, and models. All of these items can be very effective if they are used properly. Just hanging a rack of brochures up on the wall, or hanging a poster in your office is not going to be enough though. That is not using these tools properly. That is only displaying the tools. If you want these items to be effective in your patient education program you have to learn how to use them.

Let us start by writing about brochures. What types of brochures should you include inside of your office? How many of them are necessary for you to place in the office? You should stock the types of brochures that best represent the type of practice you have chosen to operate. Earlier in this book we discussed information about practice types. It is important for you to select brochure titles that are congruent with the practice type that you have subscribed to. If you have decided to specialize in the area of pediatrics, you will want to have brochures that focus on chiropractic for kids. A personal injury practice will most likely have brochures that focus on automobile accidents or whiplash injuries. The same holds true for geriatric practices and an office that has been set up to accommodate a family wellness clientele. There are numerous companies that offer a large selection of different brochure titles. Brochures are inexpensive and most companies will send you free samples so you can read through their content before you decide to purchase them. We recommend that you shop around, get some samples, and only choose titles that fit within your office mission. There is no limit to the number you can have. You can even rotate your titles every month or two in order to keep the information fresh.

Now that you have selected your brochure titles, you have to know how to utilize them. Like we stated earlier, there is a difference between displaying and effectively using brochures.

First, you must make sure that you are familiar with the content of any brochure that you place in your office. A brochure stands a much better chance of being read if you, the doctor, personally hand out the publication to your patient. The chances of being read are even greater if you open up the brochure, point to or circle a certain section, and tell the patient that you would like him or her to pay particular attention to that specific section. When your patient returns for the next visit, you will have another opportunity to educate by asking the patient if you can answer any questions he or she may have about the publication. This is much more effective than just sending a patient home with eight or nine different brochures. Always make the educational process memorable. In this situation you can also make it very personal by hand selecting one or two titles and actually giving it to the patient with a section or two marked and then doing the follow up on the next visit.

While we are on the subject of brochures we would like to also mention that it is a very good idea to have a publication about your office. You can make this yourself on almost any desktop publishing software and have the brochures printed at an office supply store for a minimal investment. These make great introductions for new or potential patients and are great handouts at health screenings.

Posters for your office should also be selected with the practice type that you have chosen in mind. They should be visible in the waiting room, exam rooms, x-ray rooms, and anywhere else that patients will spend time in your office. Use them as a way to start a chiropractic conversation. A poster of the phases of subluxation degeneration comes in very handy during your report of findings presentation. Use it to compare the patient's radiographs with one of the phases of degeneration. This becomes a very powerful tool and a very powerful motivator when a patient sees that their problem did not just happen overnight. Use a poster that illustrates posture in order to point out some of the findings of a patient's exam or to point out what to look for in a spouse or a child. The educational possibilities here are endless as long as you use the posters and not just display them.

Models are another very useful educational tool. No office should ever be without a model spine. This should be used in your two-five minute new patient orientation, your report of findings, your health talk, or any other time you feel a patient needs a more thorough, visual explanation of what you are discussing. There is no better tool on the market to show what a vertebral subluxation looks like and how very little movement it takes to impinge a nerve. You should also use your model spine to show a patient how many subluxations you have detected and where and how you will be making adjustments to correct the problems.

TABLE TALK

What you say to your patients while they are on the adjusting table can also have a great impact. If you are just talking about the weather or the last movie you saw, you are wasting a valuable educational moment. Take advantage of this time by making good "table talk." An easy style of table talk to do is to simply tell the patient what you are doing as you are doing it. During a leg check, you might say, "Your left leg is short but when you turn your head to the left, your legs become balanced. I'll be adjusting you here today."

Another style of table talk that works great is to coach and congratulate. With this style, you coach the patient through the adjustment and immediately congratulate the patient after the adjustment. You would be surprised how well this technique works. It also helps to keep the patient at ease because the individual will have immediate feed back that the adjustment that you just delivered was successful. This style might sound something like this. "Okay Bill, take a deep breath in, and then let it all the way out for me, let your shoulders relax—adjust— fantastic. That was a great adjustment." You do not have to be too animated when you congratulate the patient. Just say it as a matter of fact. "That was a great adjustment." Then move on with your exam. We have found this style to be incredibly powerful. Your patients will be a little apprehensive and not sure of what to expect (especially if they are new to chiropractic.) But, when you, their doctor, the expert, explains to them that the adjustment went just as you expected, they will be more at ease and they will have more confidence in you. It is a win-win situation.

It is okay to have the occasional weather, sports, or movie comment but you should always try to work in some chiropractic table talk on each visit. Keep your conversations balanced and be personable but get in the habit of practicing some good table talk skills.

RECALL CARDS

Patient recall cards can also be used for education purposes. These are simply little post cards with either a preprinted or hand written message on them. We recommend using recall cards to stay in touch with your patients in between visits. This tool applies more to patients who have been coming to you for a while and now their visits are spaced out over a couple of weeks. This also is applicable to patients who are supposed to be coming in for visits and have missed an appointment or two. Sending these patients a post card is sometimes all it takes to keep them on track and keep them regular with their appointments. Write a simple hand written message such as, "Following through on your plan of care will get you the best results. Please call our office to reschedule your appointment." This is probably one of the least expensive and effective ways to stay in touch with your patients. If you have a patient's e-mail address you can do the same thing electronically and it will not cost you a cent for postage. Keep in mind that not every patient will respond. No matter how hard you try, some patients will not return until another crisis develops in their life. This tool, however, is so low cost it is almost foolish not to try it. In addition, the patient will know you are trying to do what is best for their health care. We would like to write one last comment on using patient recall cards. Make sure that you document in the patient's file that you sent out a recall card and the date that you sent it out. This can be done by simply writing the date on the patient's travel card or file folder and writing the words, "recall card."

In summary, your patient education program should be an ongoing process. You cannot expect your patients to get the big idea of chiropractic after just one health talk or after just one newsletter article. Their education will not happen all at once but will occur over time. Be patient with them. Never stop trying to educate your patients. Most importantly you should never give up. Be persistent, relentless and keep in mind that in this game slow and steady eventually wins the race.

The Grand Opening

Getting ready to open the doors to your practice can be both exciting and stressful. Your grand opening event should be one that attracts as much attention to you and your office as possible. With some careful planning, you can launch your practice with a very attention getting grand opening celebration.

You should begin planning your grand opening as soon as you sign the lease to your office. The more planning you put into it, the more successful it will be. Remember, your goal for the grand opening is to attract attention. You can begin by simply stopping into all of the neighboring businesses in the town where you will be practicing. Introduce yourself as a new chiropractor in town and let everyone know where you will be practicing. Make sure you have an ample supply of business cards on hand. Give your business cards to everyone you meet. Write a little note on the back of the card. "Hope to see you at my grand opening." You should also try to collect as many business cards as possible from the people you are meeting. You will probably feel a lot like a politician and it probably will not be your most favorite activity but it is important. There is something to be said for a face to face meeting, a smile, and a handshake. It also lets everyone in town get a chance to meet you and see that you are just like them, friendly, and approachable. People you meet may not think that they need your services right now. But, if they ever do, they will remember you as that nice doctor who stopped in to say hello and invited them to a grand opening.

The next step in the planning process of your grand opening is to figure out how you want to run the event and what your guests will be doing. Are they just coming in for a tour of your office and facilities? Will you be offering spinal screenings? Will you provide door prizes? How about entertainment and decorations for the occasion? Will your guests find out information about you and the services you provide? The answer to all of these questions is of course, yes! You will want to do all of these things to the degree that your budget will allow. You can run a successful grand opening on a shoestring budget or you can spend a lot of money on the campaign. That decision is up to you. We are both advocates of a low overhead, low cost practice. You can still impress and look professional while keeping the costs down to a minimum. Office tours and spinal screenings will not cost you a dime. Decorations can range anywhere from balloons and streamers to extravagant flower arrangements, search lights, and giant helium filled outdoor attractions. We suggest you spend your money wisely.

Now let us get down to the details. Give each of your guests something to take home. Chiropractic literature in the form of brochures, one page handouts, or fact sheets are excellent choices. There are several good books out on the market about chiropractic that are written specifically for the lay person. Check with the publisher to see if they will offer you a discount if you purchase the books in volume. If your budget allows, these publications would make great take home gifts as well. Even if your budget will not permit you to buy enough for everyone, you could acquire just a few books and use them as a door prize to a contest.

A fact sheet about the doctor is an absolute must. You can

create this yourself with your home computer and a digital camera. This is essentially a short biography of you. Include your schooling, licensing, special areas of expertise, techniques you are proficient in, areas of practice you plan to specialize in, and any other pertinent information you want people to know about yourself. Be sure to include the services you plan on providing (family care, pediatric care, rehabilitation, etc.) Include a picture of yourself and all of your office contact information. The information on this fact sheet will be similar to the information you might include on your office brochure but will be more about you and your qualifications rather than your clinic and its services.

Another great idea is to offer door prizes. As we have already mentioned, a book about chiropractic makes a great door prize. Another great door prize is a gift certificate for a complimentary spinal exam at your office. You can place a dollar value and time limit on this if you wish and you should give out several of these throughout the course of the day. Some doctors have even offered gift certificates for complimentary exams to the first fifty people that show up to the grand opening. This is a great way to entice people to return to your office and get under care. Run your door prize giveaway just like a raffle contest. Give everyone who shows up at your office a numbered ticket (you can buy raffle tickets by the role at most office supply stores) and announce that you will be drawing a winning number every fifteen or twenty minutes. This will cause people to stick around long enough to take in everything about your office. It will give you time to conduct spinal screenings, pass out literature and talk with quite a few of your guests.

Serve refreshments. Nothing brings in a crowd like free food!

Whether you serve cookies and juice, coffee and donuts, pizza, sandwiches, or hot dogs and hamburgers, having food on hand at your event is necessary. Some people will come to your event just because you are giving free food away. That is good. Remember, your goal is to attract attention and drive traffic to your new office. Serve refreshments and you will have people eating right out of your hands (we could not resist that one.)

Now that you have planned your event right down to the menu, it is time to let the media in on the secret. Send out press releases. You have no guarantee that the newspapers will print your release but send them out anyway. Newspapers do end up printing quite a few press release articles. Send out a release about four weeks in advance of your grand opening and then send another one out about two weeks later. Also you should invite members of the media to your event.

You should also invite the mayor of your town. Call the mayor's office and introduce yourself as a new doctor starting a business in town. When the mayor shows up at your office you should also plan on having a ribbon cutting ceremony and have the mayor and yourself take part in the event. Mayors love to take part in these ceremonies because they know that a picture will be taken and placed in the newspaper. In many instances, the mayor's office will even help you set up the ribbon cutting ceremony and will contact the media for you.

Do you remember all those business cards that you collected when you were introducing yourself to neighboring businesses in your town? Send out a hand written invitation to each person who gave you a card. Write something about how nice it was to meet that individual and that you would greatly appreciate seeing the person at your grand opening.

On the day of your actual event, you will want to collect as many names and addresses of the people that attend as possible. One way to accomplish this is to simply have everyone that shows up sign a guest book when entering your office. Make sure that there is enough room in your guest book for a name and an address. This will help you to build a mailing list immediately for your newsletter that you will be writing. After the grand opening you should send a thank you letter to everyone who registered. Keep the letter short and to the point. "Thanks for attending our grand opening and helping to make it such a success. I look forward to serving you and your family for many years to come."

We should probably mention that you will want to enlist the help of a few friends and family members to ensure that everything runs in an organized manner on your big day. You will need someone to help with people coming in; getting them registered and passing out raffle tickets and other information. You will need someone else to help out with traffic flow, moving people in to be screened, conducting the tour of your office, etc. You will need someone to handle refreshments and door prizes as well.

During your event, have someone take pictures. Take pictures of you screening spines, shaking hands with the mayor, and just some candid shots throughout the day. Write a little caption to each picture and submit the films to the local media as a future press release about your ceremony. This is just one final attempt to grab free publicity for your office after the grand opening has taken place.

These are the basic steps that you will need to follow in order to run a successful grand opening celebration. Keep in mind that there is always a tremendous amount of room for your own creativity to shine through. Let your imagination start to work. Create a successful grand opening event and in no time at all your practice will be up and running.

Printed in the United States
845700003B